41 Active Learning Strategies for the Inclusive Classroom

Grades 6–12

This book is dedicated to the memory of my parents, Phyllis and Abby Schwartz, who would have gotten the biggest kick out of seeing this book in print; you are missed.

Linda Schwartz Green

This book is dedicated to my sisters, Ann Marie and Donna, for their unwavering support and love no matter what time, what place, or how busy. I couldn't have done it without you. . . . I will always be grateful!

Diane Casale-Giannola

41 Active Learning Strategies for the Inclusive Classroom

Grades 6-12

Diane Casale-Giannola
Linda Schwartz Green

CORWIN
A SAGE Company

FOR INFORMATION:

Corwin
A SAGE Company
2455 Teller Road
Thousand Oaks, California 91320
www.corwin.com

SAGE Publications Ltd.
1 Oliver's Yard
55 City Road
London, EC1Y 1SP
United Kingdom

SAGE Publications India Pvt. Ltd.
B 1/I 1 Mohan Cooperative Industrial Area
Mathura Road, New Delhi 110 044
India

SAGE Publications Asia-Pacific Pte. Ltd.
3 Church Street
#10-04 Samsung Hub
Singapore 049483

Acquisitions Editor: Jessica Allan
Associate Editor: Allison Scott
Editorial Assistant: Lisa Whitney
Permissions Editor: Karen Ehrmann
Project Editor: Veronica Stapleton
Copy Editor: Pam Schroeder
Typesetter: Hurix Systems
Proofreader: Scott Oney
Cover Designer: Michael Dubowe

Printed in the United States of America.

Library of Congress Cataloging-in-Publication Data

Casale-Giannola, Diane.

41 active learning strategies for the inclusive classroom, grades 6-12 / Diane Casale-Giannola, Linda Schwartz Green.

p. cm.

Includes bibliographical references and index.

ISBN 978-1-4129-9397-5 (pbk.)

1. Active learning. 2. Education, Secondary. 3. Inclusive education. I. Green, Linda Schwartz. II. Title. III. Title: Forty-one active learning strategies for the inclusive classroom, grades 6-12.

LB1027.23.C22 2012
371.9′046—dc23

2012011685

This book is printed on acid-free paper.

12 13 14 15 16 10 9 8 7 6 5 4 3 2 1

Contents

Preface

This book, *41 Active Learning Strategies for the Inclusive Classroom, Grades 6–12,* is the sequel to our first, *40 Active Learning Strategies for the Inclusive Classroom, Grades K–5,* which was designed to support diverse learners at the elementary level. Much of the impetus for our second book came from teachers and preservice teachers we have worked with over the years. They have frequently raised concerns that it can be even more difficult for secondary teachers to support diverse student populations in inclusive settings. In workshops we have conducted and classes we have taught, teachers and students often begin discussions with "How do I . . .?" This book attempts to answer these questions with many concrete strategies and applications.

The strategies in this book have been developed to address the needs of the adolescent learner. Our intent is to make lesson preparation more effective by offering teachers several active, learning-based strategies to support learning objectives. Strategies can be adapted and modified as needed.

The topics we list in each strategy are merely starting points, suggestions to help you visualize how the strategies might be used. Feel free to take these strategies and run with them, to infuse your own expertise and content knowledge, and to use them as best meets the needs of your students and your curriculum.

We believe these active learning strategies effectively support secondary school learning and will inspire and motivate teachers and students alike.

Based on the positive feedback we received from the publication of *40 Active Learning Strategies for the Inclusive Classroom, Grades K–5,* we have organized this book to include the following:

- A modified and expanded first chapter discusses the research and describes inclusion challenges at the secondary level and characteristics of the adolescent learner. It also provides the foundation and historical context of inclusive practice.
- The second chapter addresses the efficacy of using active learning for upper grades.
- The fifth chapter contains 31 completely new strategies designed to address the needs of the adolescent learner. Ten strategies from the first book have been revised with examples and vignettes that reflect middle school and high school curriculum and standards.

Acknowledgments

We would like to acknowledge each other, again, for our equal partnership, humor, and shared commitment to active learning and student success—we are so lucky to be working together.

To Jessica Allan, our editor, thanks for believing in us and for all of your help. We are grateful.

To Pam Schroeder, copy editor extraordinaire, you have made the copy editing process a pleasure. We appreciate your perspective, your professionalism, and most of all your patience.

We thank Corwin Press, and everyone who worked with us, for the opportunity and for continued support.

We would like to acknowledge Centenary College and Rider University for their support in our professional and creative endeavors.

Many thanks to Judi Ricucci, an inspiring teacher and amazing friend; for Linda, your support has been priceless throughout this entire journey—huge thanks for being there and freely sharing your ideas and professional expertise and experience—here's to continued walks and talks.

To Simon Saba, thank for you helping us with tech issues, always with a smile, without ever asking why we can't figure out how to do it ourselves.

To Deeta Fiorentino, for your willingness to read strategies and offer suggestions. Much appreciated.

To EDU 3034 at Centenary College, Fall 2011, the first class Linda taught using our own book as the text, for your total enthusiasm, making the experience such a positive one. Thanks for all of the suggestions and opinions that helped us to shape Book 2. Who knows what the front cover would have actually looked like without your honest feedback?

Thank you to our current and former colleagues, the teachers we have worked with, and all of our students whose ideas have helped to shape our own—we have learned from you.

To our students at Centenary College and Rider University who have used our first book and tried out the strategies with your own students, we thank you; it is still a thrill when we get an e-mail telling us which strategy you used, how the students responded, and how much they learned—we never get tired of those e-mails.

To Debra Stoller and Bonnie Crisco for the inspiration from active learning experiences in your classes (especially FacePlace and Philosophical Chairs) at Monroe Township Middle School. Thank you for motivating and engaging our hard-to-reach teen learners!

To Steven McConville, thank you for spending many hours sharing your insights and experiences from high school to develop more active learning strategies for this publication.

To Victoria Giannola, who shared her insights, her experiences, and even her homework to inspire many of the strategies and helped us to know the adolescent learner firsthand! For Diane, there was no greater support or inspiration that helped make this book become a reality! Thank you for your input, your honesty, and your creative spirit!

And, to our families with love—you are the most important part of everything.

From Diane Casale-Giannola

Thank you Francesca, Christian, and Victoria for being my greatest inspiration and motivation. I am so fortunate to have you. You are the very best kids that I ever did see! There is no success in my life without you.

From Linda Schwartz Green

To my husband Marc: 41 and 41, fabulous! May the second 41 achieve even a small measure of the success that the first 41 has already achieved! And thank you for your continued love and support.

To my daughter Jessica who is stronger than she even realizes—you go girl, and thanks for your enthusiasm and marketing suggestions and chicken soup.

To my son Adam, thank you for your sense of humor, your enthusiasm, and just for being you (and for your marketing ideas as well).

To daughter-in-law Nia, so glad that you are part of our lives.

And to continued adventures with all four of you.

PUBLISHER'S ACKNOWLEDGMENTS

Corwin wishes to acknowledge the following peer reviewers for their editorial insight and guidance.

Donna Adkins
Teacher
Perritt Primary
Arkadelphia, AR

Rachel Aherns
Instructional Strategist I
Westridge Elementary
West Des Moines, IA

Jim Hoogheem
Retired Principal
Osseo Area Schools
Maple Grove, MN

Rui Kang
Assistant Professor
Georgia College & State University
Milledgeville, GA

Cheryl Moss
Special Education Teacher
Gilbert Middle School
Ames, IA

Patti Palmer
Sixth Grade Language Arts Teacher
Wynford School
Bucyrus, OH

Amanda M. Rudolph
Associate Professor
Stephen F. Austin State University
Nacogdoches, TX

About the Authors

Dr. Diane Casale-Giannola is a dedicated educator. She is a native New Yorker who has a passion for culture and international experiences, teaching in the United States and abroad. While she has taught from preschool to graduate school, she has also worked in many leadership roles, including assistant principal, director, and principal. Diane has several degrees. She earned a BA in English and Secondary Education and an MS in Special Education from the State University of New York at Albany. Then, she went on to earn an Advanced Certificate in Education Administration and Supervision from Brooklyn College and a doctorate from New York University in Education, Administration, and Leadership.

Currently a professor at Rider University, Dr. Casale-Giannola has been recognized as the Distinguished Teacher of the Year. Other educational endeavors include professional development, consulting, and speaking at educational conferences nationally and internationally. She is published in many professional journals and now has two books published with Corwin Press to support teachers and engage students. Her research interests and publications focus on supporting diverse learners through inclusion, global education, and effective practice. Diane is committed to lifelong learning and believes the recipe for success is one part knowledge, one part passion, and two parts humor. Diane is committed to making a difference in the lives of others and improving a diverse world.

Dr. Linda Schwartz Green has been involved in the field of special education since the beginning of her career, teaching in public school, starting the first resource room in her district, and working as a liaison between school and family, before becoming a full-time faculty member at Centenary College. As her children were growing up and people asked what their mom did, the response was always, "She teaches teachers how to teach." That pretty much sums it up. She is currently a professor at Centenary College where she is the director of the Students With Disabilities certification program, has developed the MA in Special Education, and serves as director of the special education graduate program. She received the Centenary College Distinguished Teacher Award. Dr. Green has also been an educational consultant, preparing and implementing numerous workshops on a variety of topics related to special education for teachers and for parents, and she regularly presents at national special education conferences.

She received her undergraduate degree in English and English Education from the University of Bridgeport, an MA in Special Education and Reading from Eastern New Mexico University, and a PhD in Special Education and Psychological and Cultural Studies from the University of Nebraska. Growing up in New York City and continuing her education in Connecticut, New Mexico, and Nebraska sparked not only her love of learning but also her quest to visit every state in the union (only four more to go).

Together Drs. Casale-Giannola and Green have published a companion book, *40 Active Learning Strategies for the Inclusive Classroom, Grades K–5,* which contains innovative lesson-planning ideas for younger students.

1

Inclusion at the Secondary Level

THE BLUEBERRY STORY: THE TEACHER GIVES THE BUSINESSMAN A LESSON

"If I ran my business the way you people operate your schools, I wouldn't be in business very long!"

I stood before an auditorium filled with outraged teachers who were becoming angrier by the minute. My speech had entirely consumed their precious 90 minutes of in-service. Their initial icy glares had turned to restless agitation. You could cut the hostility with a knife. I represented a group of business people dedicated to improving public schools. I was an executive at an ice cream company that became famous in the middle 1980s when People Magazine chose our blueberry as the "Best Ice Cream in America."

I was convinced of two things. First, public schools needed to change; they were archaic selecting and sorting mechanisms designed for the industrial age and out of step with the needs of our emerging "knowledge society." Second, educators were a major part of the problem: they resisted change, hunkered down in their feathered nests, protected by tenure and shielded by a bureaucratic monopoly. They needed to look to business. We knew how to produce quality. Zero defects! TQM! Continuous improvement!

In retrospect, the speech was perfectly balanced—equal parts ignorance and arrogance. As soon as I finished, a woman's hand shot up. She appeared polite, pleasant—she was, in fact, a razor-edged, veteran, high school English teacher who had been waiting to unload. She began quietly, "We are told, sir, that you manage a company that makes good ice cream." I smugly replied, "Best ice cream in America, Ma'am."

(Continued)

(Continued)

"How nice," she said. "Is it rich and smooth?"

"Sixteen percent butterfat," I crowed.

"Premium ingredients?" she inquired.

"Super-premium! Nothing but triple A." I was on a roll. I never saw the next line coming.

"Mr. Vollmer," she said, leaning forward with a wicked eyebrow raised to the sky, "when you are standing on your receiving dock and you see inferior shipments of blueberries arrive, what do you do?"

In the silence of that room, I could hear the trap snap. . . . I was dead meat, but I wasn't going to lie. "I send them back."

"That's right!" she barked, "and we can never send back our blueberries. We take them big, small, rich, poor, gifted, exceptional, abused, frightened, confident, homeless, rude, and brilliant. We take them with ADHD, junior rheumatoid arthritis, and English as their second language. We take them all! Every one! And that, Mr. Vollmer, is why it's not a business. It's school!"

In an explosion, all 290 teachers, principals, bus drivers, aides, custodians, and secretaries jumped to their feet and yelled, "Yeah! Blueberries! Blueberries!"

And so began my long transformation. Since then, I have visited hundreds of schools. I have learned that a school is not a business. Schools are unable to control the quality of their raw material, they are dependent upon the vagaries of politics for a reliable revenue stream, and they are constantly mauled by a howling horde of disparate, competing customer groups that would send the best CEO screaming into the night.

None of this negates the need for change. We must change what, when, and how we teach to give all children maximum opportunity to thrive in a post-industrial society. But educators cannot do this alone; these changes can occur only with the understanding, trust, permission, and active support of the surrounding community. For the most important thing I have learned is that schools reflect the attitudes, beliefs, and health of the communities they serve, and therefore, to improve public education means more than changing our schools, it means changing America.

 Jamie Robert Vollmer, a businessman and attorney, now works as a motivational speaker and consultant to increase community support for public schools. He can be reached at Jamie@jamievollmer.com.

This true story speaks to the very heart of education: It is our job; our responsibility; and our ethical, moral, and professional obligation to educate every one of the students who come through our doors. Teachers work to maximize the potential in every student. How to best accomplish this is the issue. Inclusion, differentiated instruction, learning styles, learning modalities, multiple intelligences, and blueberries are different concepts related to a common goal.

Diverse students are included in our classrooms, and teachers need a variety of methods and strategies to support students' strengths and address their needs. Inclusion teachers need to be equipped with the expertise and strategies to motivate students and enhance student performance and learning outcomes.

The very best teachers share ideas, pool their resources, and are always looking for another creative way to structure a lesson or to motivate a reluctant learner. It is impossible for any one person to possess the knowledge, ability, and creativity to meet the needs of every student in the classroom, but each of us continues to strive toward this goal. Teachers consistently seek out methods to positively affect student growth. This book is one such resource that will build your repertoire of strategies to support and engage students of varying needs in the inclusive secondary classroom. Please take this journey with us.

DEFINITION AND RESEARCH

Inclusion is the term used to describe the education of students with disabilities in general education settings (Mastropieri & Scruggs, 2000). Inclusion is based on the philosophy that all students with disabilities have a right to be educated in a general education setting with appropriate support and services to enable them to succeed. In comparison to elementary education, there has been less attention but greater needs at the secondary level for effective inclusion practices. Heightened secondary inclusion challenges include but are not limited to increased student diversity, high-stakes testing with increased numbers of individuals with disabilities participating, increased content area instruction, new requirements for highly qualified teachers, and expectations to meet higher standards for all students (Dieker, 2007; Sabornie & deBettencourt, 2009). General and special educators are now legally accountable for diverse student performance. Shifts in the roles and responsibilities of teachers, especially at the secondary level, necessitate that they modify their planning and instruction to meet the needs of the inclusive classroom (Muraski, 2009).

Accountability no longer lies with the special educator alone (Smith, Palloway, Patton, & Dowdy, 2006). Inclusion recognizes that all students are learners who benefit from meaningful, challenging, and appropriate curricula and differentiated instruction techniques that address their unique strengths and needs (Salend, 2005). Effective inclusion is the result of a collaborative effort of general educators, parents, related service providers, and all school community members who share roles in the successful education of students with special needs. Salend (2005) and Smith et al. (2006) summarize the advantages of inclusion when students who are classified are included in general education curricula and can benefit socially and academically without facing the stigma of segregated or pull-out classrooms. Standards for behavior and instruction are higher, and students with classifications have more opportunity to reach higher standards and become independent learners. Studies also indicate that students without disabilities can benefit from inclusive settings. Findings reveal academic performance is equal or superior to comparative groups of students educated in noninclusive settings, and students with severe disabilities do not significantly limit or interrupt instructional time for nondisabled peers in inclusive settings. Friendships and awareness of diversity are also benefits of an inclusive classroom for individuals without disabilities.

THE INCLUSIVE CLASSROOM AT THE SECONDARY LEVEL: WHO ARE WE TEACHING?

The inclusive classroom includes students with and without disabilities. Diverse student learners are identified, and the characteristics of learners are considered in the planning and instructional process. Students with special education classifications, served under the Individuals With Disabilities Act (IDEA), include those with the following classifications: autism, communication disorders, deaf-blindness, hearing impairments, other health impairments, emotional disabilities, specific learning disabilities, cognitive impairments, traumatic brain injuries, and visual impairments.

At the secondary level, the majority of students with special education classifications have high-incidence disabilities. They include learning disabilities, high-functioning intellectual disabilities, emotional disturbances, and traumatic brain injury. Some students with high-functioning autism may also fit within the category of mild disabilities and are served in secondary general education settings. Attention Deficit Hyperactivity Disorder (ADHD) is not recognized as a disability category, but more students with ADHD are found in secondary inclusion classrooms, sometimes classified as *other health impaired* (Hallahan, Kauffman, & Pullen, 2010).

Other instances of classroom diversity not associated with disabilities but important in the inclusive academic and social learning experience are cultural and linguistic diversity, such as English Language Learners; at-risk students, such as students with sociocultural disadvantages and limited experiences; gifted and talented students; and students who exhibit specific skills or abilities substantially above others of their age and grade level. Even without a classification, "average" students come to the classroom with unique abilities, needs, and interests.

THE ADOLESCENT LEARNER

Who are adolescent learners, and why is it so challenging to meet their needs? For the purpose of this book, we are targeting students in middle and high school, typically ages 11 to 18, the early adolescent and adolescent years. It is not surprising that the middle school years, sometimes referred to as the wonder years, describe a period when individuals experience more growth than at any other time in their lives since infancy. The following characteristics of adolescents emerge at the middle school level and make them unique learners: the need for autonomy and independence, the need for socialization and social acceptance, curiosity, and the quest for adventure and sensitivity. They are vulnerable and emotional. As adolescents are developing their personal identities, self-esteem and social acceptance are critical (Saylers & McKee, 2002).

Adolescents have specific learning characteristics that have implications for instructional planning and classroom learning. First, they prefer active engagement in the learning process (Checkley, 2005; Lent, 2006; Saylers & McKee, 2002). They are also critical thinkers who begin to reflect, creating and finding relationships among similar ideas and concepts as well as cause and effect (Saylers & McKee, 2002; Wilson & Horch, 2002). Adolescent learners respond to explicit modeling, practice, organization, and structure (Gore, 2010; Swanson, 2001;

Swanson & Deshler, 2003). An active learning environment is preferred as adolescent learners have limited attention spans and are easily bored (Dieker, 2007; Karten, 2009; Nunly, 2006).

Sabornie and deBettencourt (2009) identify the common characteristics of adolescents, with classifications, who are students in inclusive classrooms at the secondary school level:

1. Academic Deficits—This refers to poor basic skills. Literacy, reading and writing, represents the greatest academic area of need. Math and problem solving are also concerns. Academic deficits are the hallmark of students with learning problems at the secondary level (Hallahan et al., 2010).

2. Cognitive Deficits—Adolescent learners passively approach learning. They have memory and attention problems that hinder mastery of content. These students do not have the cognitive strategies to support their own learning processes.

3. Social Interaction Deficits—Students with mild disabilities have a difficult time being accepted and developing peer relationships. Even suicide and depression has increased significantly among this population, unfortunately becoming a leading cause of death for this age group.

4. Study Skills Deficits—Studying and test taking pose challenges for adolescent learners. They make little use of cognitive strategies but will perform significantly better when presented with strategies to organize and interact with material (Lenz & Deshler, 2004).

5. Organization Deficits (sometimes connected with study skills)—This is another concern for adolescents. They have trouble note-taking, organizing their materials, and keeping up with the school agenda while navigating middle and high school environments.

6. Motivation Problems (often connected with passive learning)—Students with mild disabilities may exhibit learned helplessness and believe academic success is beyond their control. This may be attributed to years of failure. Without taking active roles in learning, most will not succeed.

While many of these characteristics are evident early in a student's learning career, they become more evident as years pass and the gap increases. As students enter secondary school, the focus shifts to content instruction at a faster pace, which can be daunting for adolescents with cognitive, social, or emotional needs.

HELPING TEACHERS MEET THE INCLUSION CHALLENGE

Although general education teachers typically support the concept of inclusive education, they often find themselves unsupported and ill equipped to provide effective instruction and support for diverse students in the inclusive classroom (Bender, 2008; Mastropieri & Scruggs, 2000). Teachers are often hungry for strategies to support students with disabilities in the general education classroom

(Bender, 2008). Even when teachers have positive attitudes toward inclusion, knowledge of how to adapt instruction, and the desire to make instructional changes, they still do not significantly alter their traditional whole-group instructional approaches (Friend & Bursuck, 2002). As coteaching becomes more common in the inclusive classroom, two teachers have even more opportunity to provide "unique and high-involvement instructional strategies to engage all students in ways that are not possible when only one teacher is present" (p. 110). Such creative options enhance learning for all students, not just those with disabilities (Friend, 2010).

Active learning is a viable option that can accommodate diverse student needs in the inclusive classroom, meeting student and curricula challenges (Udvari-Solner & Kluth, 2008). Adolescent learners benefit from active learning experiences as they become engaged and motivated to participate in the learning process (Gore, 2010; Maday, 2008; Lent, 2006; Reilly, 2002; Saylers & McKee, 2002; Swanson & Deshler, 2003). Brain-based learning and motivational research support such strategies because they provide opportunities to engage students in the learning process. Active learning strategies can be instrumental in the teacher's quest to create positive learning experiences and outcomes. This book provides an opportunity for teachers to explore a multitude of active learning strategies that support students academically and socially in inclusive settings.

WHAT IS ACTIVE LEARNING?

Active learning is the intentional opportunity for students to engage in the learning process. It connects learners to the content through movement, reflection, or discussion, making students the center of the learning process as they take the initiative to learn. It can be behavioral or cognitive, supporting a variety of instructional objectives from recall through synthesis (Green & Casale-Giannola, 2011). Silberman (1996) addresses the question of what makes learning active. He explains, "When learning is active, students do most of the work. They use their brains, study ideas, solve problems, and apply what they learn. Active learning is fast-paced, fun, supportive, and personally engaging" (p. ix). Often students are out of their seats, moving about, and thinking aloud. Active learning engages and motivates students while enhancing understanding and performance (Guillaume, Yopp, & Yopp, 2007; Silberman, 1996, 2006; Udvari-Solner & Kluth, 2008; Zmuda, 2008). It is important to make learning active because, to learn something well, a student needs to hear it, see it, ask questions about it, and discuss it with others. Above all, students need to do it (Silberman, 1996).

Research studies report that many active learning strategies are equally effective for mastering content when compared with lecture formats; what is significant is that active learning strategies are superior to lectures for student achievement in thinking and writing. Cognitive research also supports the premise that student learning styles are best addressed with multiple instructional methodologies (Bonwell & Eisen, 1991). Bonwell and Eisen, educators who popularized the term *active learning*, describe its general characteristics as follows:

- Students are involved in more than listening.
- Instruction emphasizes the development of students' skills rather than just transmitting information.

- Students develop higher-order thinking skills (analysis, synthesis, evaluation).
- Students are engaged in activities (e.g., reading, discussing, and writing).
- Students explore their own attitudes and values.

Pedagogy that includes interactive teaching strategies leads to education for sustainable learning (Corney & Reid, 2007). Teachers who embrace experiential learning can use active or hands-on experiences as methods to recognize desirable outcomes and endorse student-centered instructional approaches (Fenwick, 2001). Research has confirmed that student-centered, hands-on experiences improve construction of knowledge, comprehension, and the retention of content information.

Active learning strategies can support all levels of objectives in Bloom's Taxonomy, from knowledge and translation to evaluation and synthesis. Active learning is particularly important for application, which is necessary for learning to transfer from short-term to long-term memory and be easily retrievable. Jarolimek and Foster (1981) describe the *activity mode* of teaching as a set of strategies that involves students in learning by doing things that are meaningful and related to the topic of study. Techniques include role-playing, constructing, interpreting, preparing exhibits, processing, groupwork, and games. Active learning may also apply to inquiry modes of learning, which include techniques such as drawing conclusions, asking questions, and stating hypotheses (Wood, 2009). The strategies shared in this book are designed to actively engage students in their own learning. Alone, they are activities, but once the activities are connected to specific learning and behavioral objectives, they become strategies to support learners and achievement outcomes. This active learning concept relates directly to the Native American proverb, "I hear and I forget; I see and I remember; I do and I understand" (Wood, 2009).

BRAIN-BASED LEARNING AND THE ADOLESCENT LEARNER

Brain-imaging devices can now give researchers a look inside the brain and determine which areas are involved as it carries out certain tasks. Some of these discoveries are valuable for diagnosing medical problems, while others have implications for what educators do in schools and classrooms (Sousa, 2007). William Bender (2002) lists 10 tactics for a brain-compatible classroom, based on the accumulated research in this area, including the following:

- Structure frequent student responses.
- Pair physical movement to learning tasks.
- Use visual stimuli for increasing novelty in the learning task.
- Give students choices.
- Use students to teach each other (p. 26).

Specifically, adolescents with learning problems have trouble encoding information into their memory systems and lack basic skills and cognitions that support high-order thinking. They have to retrain their brains to make meaningful connections to newly learned concepts. "Each time a neural trace is activated, that arm of the neuron becomes stronger and easier to access the next time. . . . The brains of students with learning problems are not as efficient in making those neural traces stronger, so they need to activate the traces more frequently in order to strengthen the connections. Thus, repetition through multisensory, multirepresentational input, practice, and frequent review are necessary" (Gore, 2010, p. 25).

Adolescents, specifically, can benefit more from cooperative social learning experiences than elementary school children. It is easy to visualize elementary students waving their arms frantically, popping out of their seats and chanting "Me, me" when asked to respond to a question. It is even not surprising when one of these avid youngsters is called upon and the class finds they have nothing to say; they were just excited to participate. It is not so with adolescents who are cautious among peers to participate as image and social acceptance are critical at this stage. Cooperative learning experiences can provide opportunities to engage socially without the stress of being singled out or called to the board alone. Brain processes that create emotional stress and discomfort can interfere with knowledge connections, retrieval, and the flow of information. Creating active learning opportunities that engage adolescent learners effectively supports their emotional need to be accepted and acknowledged among their peers (Willis, 2007). Allowing students to learn collaboratively and cooperatively at this stage also supports students with a wide range of academic ability and social maturities while developing group problem-solving skills (Wilson & Horch, 2002).

Clearly, using active learning strategies that involve students directly in their own learning is compatible with what we are learning about brain function. These strategies can help to differentiate instruction and support students with and without disabilities in the classroom (Bender, 2008). Many of these strategies involve movement, which can cause the brain to release dopamine and noradrenalin, neurotransmitters that help learners feel better, increase energy levels, and assist their brains to store and retrieve information (Jensen, 2000).

INFORMATION PROCESSING

Figure 1.1 Information Processing Model

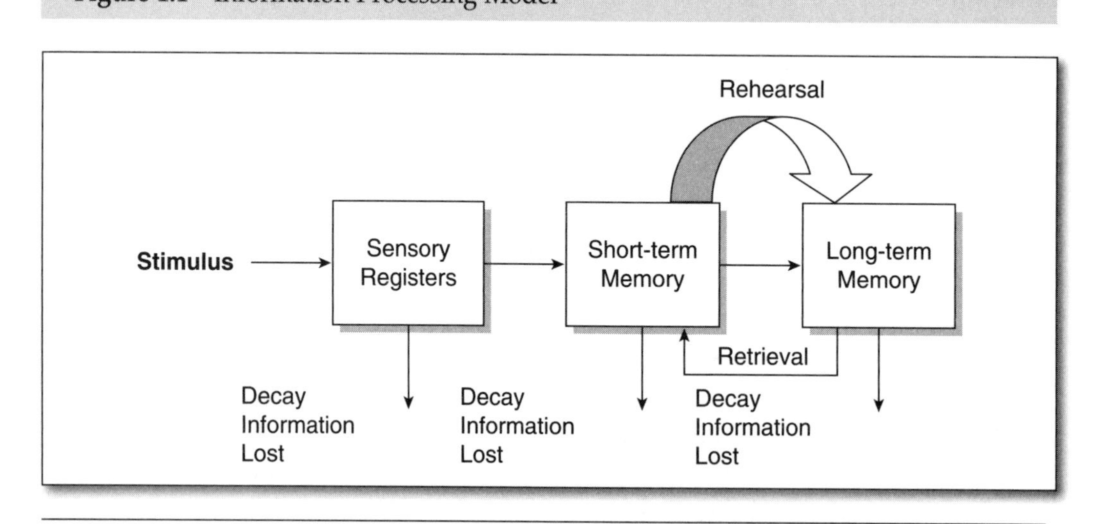

Source: Swanson (1987).

Information processing refers to how people learn new content. The information processing model in Figure 1.1 (page 8) "is an attempt to describe how sensory input is perceived, transformed, reduced, elaborated, stored, retrieved, and used" (Swanson, 1987). The stimulus is perceived by sensory registers and transferred to short-term memory. At this point, there is rehearsal of new content in order for it to be transferred to long-term memory, from which it can be retrieved (Sliva, 2004). Simply stated, learners have to do something with new information to keep it in short-term memory or transfer it to long-term memory in a meaningful way so that it can be retrieved as needed.

Think about a junk drawer you may have in your house. (Doesn't everybody have at least one in the kitchen where keys, pens, and all kinds of small objects are jumbled together?) Compare this to your silverware drawer, where each item has a place. In which drawer is it easier to find what you need quickly? Organization facilitates retrieval. In the same way, new information needs to be held in short-term memory or transferred from short-term to long-term memory in an organized manner so that the student can find and retrieve this information easily.

> If information is to be learned, it will either be transferred to and stored in long-term memory, or a strategy will be utilized to keep the information in short-term memory. Unless a strategy is used to remember this information, it will be lost in about 15 seconds. Some strategies that can be utilized to keep this information active in short-term memory are to rehearse the information, chunk it, elaborate on it, or create visual images of it. Information is then transferred from short-term memory to long-term memory where it is stored until needed. (Sliva, 2004, p. 16)

Teachers can help students make multiple brain connections to support memory. The more connections a student has to specific knowledge, the more opportunity the student has to retrieve information. There are several opportunities for students to store knowledge, including making personal connections, using multisensory application and presentation, and establishing emotional connections and connections to personal experience. When multiple regions of the brain store data, more interconnections are made, and data is cross-referenced. This cross-referencing strengthens the data into something students learn as opposed to something students just memorize (Willis, 2006).

In a meta-analysis, Swanson and Deshler (2003) identify three applications that support the learning process for adolescents with learning disabilities: (1) selecting the central process that makes the details and facts hang together and identifying relationships among concepts; (2) selecting and instructing devices that make the content more understandable and memorable; and (3) presenting content in a way that actively involves students while enhancing their learning (pp. 129–130).

Based on these findings, teachers need to be deliberate in their planning to actively engage students in the learning process while finding ways to provide advanced organization or concepts and strategies to rehearse and reinforce learning. *Rehearsing* the information refers to going over it more than once. *Chunking* it refers to dividing the information into smaller pieces or sections and studying each section. We can also chunk information in sections that relate to one another.

When we *elaborate* on new content, we describe it in more depth, often relating it to prior knowledge. *Creating a visual image* of new content can include pictures, symbols, or diagrams to help us remember. The important point is that, in order to fully learn new information, we have to become involved with the learning process, utilizing one or more strategies to promote understanding and keep the material in short-term memory or facilitate meaningful storage in long-term memory. Information processing generally takes place both unconsciously and automatically. As learners, we are not always cognizant of how and when the procedure takes place (Sliva, 2004).

As educators, it is important for us to be aware of this process and of how we can design instruction that encourages successful information processing. Including active learning strategies in instructional design is one way to accomplish this. Information from brain-based research translates into many effective classroom applications for active learning in the adolescent classroom. To hold the attention of adolescent learners, teachers can design student-centered experiences that include a full range of sensory motor experiences, including music, touch, and emotion. Providing multiple ways for students to approach learning and encourage questioning and inquiry-based instruction supports adolescent learning while building complex neuron connections within the brain (Wilson & Horch, 2002). Such applications are clearly connected to active learning strategies that can support differentiated instruction, allowing teachers to meet the diverse needs of individual students in the inclusive classroom.

CONNECTIONS TO DIFFERENTIATED INSTRUCTION

Differentiated instruction provides multiple opportunities to support diverse students in inclusive settings. It requires teachers to identify the strengths and needs of their students and possess a repertoire of strategies to support students with and without disabilities. It challenges teachers to study and think about the learning process as they find avenues to engage and motivate diverse students. It takes into account individuals' needs, readiness, interests, and learning profiles. It focuses on instruction that appeals to and engages each student (King-Shaver & Hunter, 2003).

Interest refers to curiosity and passion for a specific topic, while *learning profile* refers to a student's intelligence preferences, gender, and learning style (Tomlinson, 1999). Teachers must be ready to engage students in instruction using different learning modalities (visual, auditory, kinesthetic, or tactile), appealing to interests and degrees of complexity. Differentiated instruction focuses on the content, product, and process of learning (Tomlinson, 1999).

Tomlinson (1999) recommends teachers use students' differences as the foundation for instructional planning. When choosing activities that engage and include students, purposeful and flexible grouping is always a consideration. Visual, auditory, kinesthetic, and tactile approaches may meet the students' preferred learning modalities or support a multisensory approach. Many of the active learning strategies support students at different functioning levels and allow them to contribute their perspective in a number of ways: in written and oral communication, in groups, or individually. Choosing a strategy to support learners well means that teachers have already identified the abilities and profiles of their students and have considered content and presentation. It often means encouraging students to understand multiple viewpoints and share reflections. Providing students with choices and making connections to the interests of adolescents engages them in learning while addressing their need to show independence (Wilson & Horch, 2002). Each student is different, and the strategies in this book are designed to help educators develop a repertoire of strategies in order to meet specific student needs effectively. Although many of the strategies are movement and cooperation based (such as Ball Toss, Spider Web, Jigsaw, and Linked-In), others are individual and reflective (such as Exit Cards, Self-Reporting and Through Our Own Lens). Teachers are encouraged to adapt and modify strategies to support the differentiated needs of adolescent learners.

SUPPORTING STATE STANDARDS AND ASSESSMENTS

At a time when teachers feel overburdened and overpressured by new initiatives, standards, high-stakes assessments, and increased student needs in the classroom, the last thing a teacher needs to do is try yet another idea! However, it can be "Active learning to the rescue" as opposed to "Please! No more extra work!" Active learning strategies support objectives, standards, and assessments rather than add to them. Standards-driven instruction can be effectively aligned with differentiation and active learning to create learning experiences that make physical, emotional, and reflective connections to objectives that impact student growth and goal attainment (Gregory & Kuzmich, 2004). Active learning supports the instructional process and product of the classroom by building a community of learners who are cooperative, interactive, and brain compatible. These concepts are aligned with the research that supports standards (Benson, 2009). Standards should support the globalization of learning as teachers are committed to big ideas rather than textbook chapters and guides. Lesson choice and design should become clearer with a standards focus (Perna & Davis, 2007).

Although each state has its own academic standards, they typically include goals such as comprehension, writing proficiency, numeric operations and applications, inquiry, analysis, historical perspective, problem solving, comparing, making real-life connections, and so on. Standards set high expectations for students while keeping teachers focused on critical thinking in the learning process. Active learning strategies specifically support standards as well as academic and behavioral objectives. For example, strategies such as Traveling Teams, Round Robin, and Why and Because can be used to evaluate, synthesize, and/or make connections to different concepts.

Assessments are designed to measure what students know and what they need to learn in relation to the standards. Grades no longer evaluate what students know. Now, educators and politicians are looking at what students know in comparison to others. This does not mean that learning cannot be motivating and meaningful, but it needs to be focused with deliberate practices to support diverse learners (Benson, 2009; Perna & Davis, 2007). Teachers need to make connections between standards and student achievement, tailoring instruction to provide opportunities to reflect and apply knowledge to real-world contexts. A clear, standards-based curriculum allows for review and application without redundancy, all of which are key components of active learning (Perna & Davis, 2007).

State assessment or high-stakes testing used for promotion, rating, or placement typically brings on undue stress that can be passed from administrator to teacher to student. Families and entire communities can feel anxious and tense until the tests are over. Some teachers feel compelled to teach to the test, and you may hear comments like "We can finally teach" after assessments are administered. Certainly, statewide testing is meant to evaluate student performance, not to replace instruction, but accountability and competition in the field of education sometimes cause educators to think otherwise. Although assessments, like standards, differ among states and even districts, many of the concepts are the same.

Two of the objectives that assessments typically test include the following:

1. Basic skills including reading, writing, and mathematics
2. Subject area content knowledge

Active learning strategies can help teachers meet these two key assessment objectives. They support teachers in their efforts to teach, review, and reinforce. For example, basic skills and content knowledge can be reviewed using Traveling Teams, Face Place, and Next.

The ability to develop concepts to explain and persuade, which writing assessments often require, can be supported by activities such as Invention Convention, Barometer, and Concept Clarification, which can provide teachers with data on formative and summative objective and standard attainment, thus making student performance evaluations meaningful and generating information to guide future teaching decisions. At the same time, active learning makes dull, difficult, or repetitive material interesting and engaging.

MOTIVATING LEARNERS WITH ACTIVE LEARNING STRATEGIES

Consider the fact that, in 1926, John Dewey asked, "Why is it, in spite of the fact that teaching by pouring in, learning by passive absorption, are universally condemned, that they are still so entrenched in practice" (p. 46)? It is hard to believe how history continues to repeat itself.

Motivation refers to students' willingness to engage in lessons and learning activities. For teachers, a major goal of lesson development is to identify motivational strategies that encourage students to engage in classroom activities that meet specific educational objectives (Brophy, 1997). Engaged students investigate educational content more thoroughly (Zmuda, 2008).

Motivation affects learning. As you read, take a moment to think about your own learning. Recall a situation in which you were highly motivated to learn. Then, contrast this experience with a learning situation in which your motivation was low (or maybe nonexistent).What was the difference? Why? How can we use what we know about our own learning experiences to shape our teaching and encourage our students to be active participants in their own learning?

When students report high levels of motivation to learn, four factors are generally present: the opportunity to learn, facilitators who probe for student response, support for student learning through modeling, and scaffolding and evaluation. Strategies that incorporate these factors, such as the strategies in this book, result in increased student motivation and involvement. Research suggests that the transition from elementary to secondary school leaves the adolescent with specific needs. The middle school environment and adolescent development can be a mismatch for motivation in the early adolescent years. There are more rules and regulations, the relationships between teachers and students are limited, and there is little choice. All of these factors do not support the adolescent learner who seeks autonomy, independence, and a social learning experience that strengthens self-identity and self-esteem (Anderman & Maehr, 1994).

We also acknowledge that increased time, curriculum, standards, and high-stakes testing constraints have left teachers with little room to devote to process and outcome connections at the secondary school level. With the shift in focus from teaching to learning in an era of accountability, it is important to support teachers in their efforts to find motivating strategies that improve achievement for diverse learners. Uguroglu and Walberg (1979) provide substantial evidence that motivation is consistently and positively related to educational achievement. Research also clearly indicates that active learning engages and motivates diverse students in the learning process and has resulted in increased performance outcomes (Carroll & Leander, 2001; Ginsberg, 2005; Rugutt, 2004; Smart & Csapo, 2007; Wood, 2008).

Active learning can be an effective and essential instructional component of the inclusion classroom. Students with special needs who are actively involved and engaged tend to learn more and faster. Hands-on interactive learning appeals to the senses and provides a reason to learn, promotes attention to task, and may lessen negative behaviors (Choate, 2004).

The ability to motivate students is fundamental to equity in teaching and learning, and it is a core virtue of educators who successfully differentiate instruction (Tomlinson & Allan, 2000). Awareness of and respect for diversity, such as cultural differences, encourages teachers to invite the experiences, concerns, opinions, and perspectives of diverse students to be shared and valued in the learning process.

Lessons that respect diversity are especially motivating for students from low socioeconomic communities. Students will be more motivated to learn when their voices and perspectives are shared and valued and connections to personal experience are made. Learners will be more engaged by teachers who help them connect to and respect one another in the learning process (Ginsberg, 2005). Overall, teachers can redesign the teaching and learning environment by providing different learning strategies to different students and finding ways to motivate students to learn as they engage them in the active learning process (Rugutt, 2004).

Active learning strategies are not one size fits all. Each strategy shared in this book must be carefully examined to make sure it can be used to make meaningful connections to student needs, interests, and abilities while clearly connecting to lesson objectives, purposes, and appropriate state standards. Although some active learning strategies are cooperative and others are individual in nature, all provide distinct alternatives to lecturing and identify the student as the center of the learning process. Encouraging engagement and motivation ultimately enhances learner outcomes for all students.

ACCESS IS NOT ENOUGH: THE CRITICAL NEED TO ADDRESS DIVERSE STUDENT POPULATIONS

The conception of disabilities has changed dramatically in the past several hundred years in a multitude of ways. Historically, people with pronounced disabilities were, more often than not, beggars walking around with cap in hand, looking for money with which to support themselves. Hence, the term *handicapped,* derived from "cap in hand." Today, we try to include and value individuals with disabilities in society and in the education process.

As a result of recent legislation, the critical need to address diverse student populations has become more and more apparent. From 1954 to 1975, landmark legislation tried to protect and include diverse student populations in the educational process. *Brown v. Board of Education* (1954) ruled that segregation based on race and other educational factors was unconstitutional. *Hansen v. Hobsen* (1967) ruled that ability grouping or tracking violated due process and equal protection under the Constitution. In 1970, *Diana v. State Board of Education* required that students be tested in their primary language. In 1975, the Education for All Handicapped Children Act (PL 94-142) mandated that students with disabilities must receive the most appropriate services and are entitled to receive a free and appropriate public education in the least-restricted environment (LRE; Gable & Hendrickson, 2004). The LRE clause of PL 94-142 and the Regular Education Initiative (REI) from the 1980s called for the restructuring of special and general education, supporting the inclusion of at-risk students, culturally diverse students, and students with disabilities in the general education classroom (Gable & Hendrickson, 2004).

Unfortunately, many years later, students with learning differences were still excluded from the general education curriculum. Schools and teachers were not held accountable for the achievement and performance of students with special needs. In 1997, the Individuals With Disabilities Education Act (IDEA) required inclusion of individuals with disabilities in the general education curriculum, holding the general and special education teachers accountable for the achievement of students classified with special needs (Karten, 2005).

Moreover, in 2001, President George W. Bush introduced the No Child Left Behind Act (NCLB; PL 107-110), which made schools accountable for the performance of many diverse populations, including students with diverse ethnic and cultural backgrounds, students with disabilities, males and females, and students of varying socioeconomic status. Differentiated assessments are selected by specific states and schools to identify and report the Annual Yearly Progress of the school as well as the disaggregated data from diverse student groups. All student achievement must be recorded in school data, and teachers are expected to implement research-based instructional practices to support quality education for all students. Thus, in an era of inclusion and accountability, access is not enough. Educators are more responsible for the quality of instruction and diverse student population performance than ever before.

At the secondary level, federal legislation, NCLB, created an even greater need for inclusion. This act is the most significant reform connected to the Elementary and Secondary Education Act (ESEA) since its enactment in 1965. It redefined K–12 education and hoped to close the achievement gap between the majority of general education students and their minority and disadvantaged peers (Sabornie & deBettencourt, 2009). First, NCLB was another federal law introduced to support IDEA in moving students to participate more completely in the general education curriculum, and the *highly qualified* teaching criteria were established. This meant that all teachers who teach a subject area above the fifth grade level must have expertise in that content area. Special education teachers at the secondary level were no longer allowed to provide instruction for a specific content area unless those teachers were coteaching with a licensed content area educator or the special education teacher also held a license in that particular content area (Sabornie & deBettencourt, 2009). Therefore, NCLB created additional challenges at the secondary level, including shifts in teacher roles and accountability, less interaction between students with classifications and special education teachers, the identification and hiring of qualified personnel, and scheduling for in-class support or coteaching partners.

Legislation and the inclusion movement have not just relocated students from self-contained to inclusion classrooms. The movement has had a serious impact on the roles and responsibilities of teachers. General educators are responsible for the performance of growing numbers of diverse students in their classrooms. To ensure the success of students, general and special educators must work collaboratively to combine their knowledge of what to teach with the knowledge of how to teach (Choate, 2004). Educators often appreciate diverse learners in their classrooms but feel they lack the resources and expertise needed to support their learning (Bruneau-Balderrama, 1997; Mastropieri, 2001; Snyder, 1999). Teachers need the skills and experience to meet the specific needs of different students in the classroom, so they feel empowered to teach successfully (Cook, 2002; O'Shea, 1999). Rather than dispense knowledge, an educator should guide and facilitate interaction to encourage learners to question and challenge ideas, opinions, and conclusions. Active learning has numerous positive attributes and is independent of age, cross-cultural, easy to acquire, and independent of measures of intelligence (Jensen, 2001).

THE BEGINNING

At the beginning of this chapter, we invited you to take a journey with us. We hope you're ready. Right now, if you choose to come along, you'll need a few things:

- An understanding of the characteristics of adolescent learners and how this clearly informs instructional design

- An understanding of your inclusive student population (consider classification, ages, interests, learning styles, dynamics, abilities, strengths, needs, etc.)
- Curriculum—goals and objectives for specific units and lessons—and standards that inform the curriculum
- A willingness to adapt and be flexible
- A willingness to reflect
- Motivation to excite and engage your students with your own enthusiasm for teaching and learning
- A good travel partner—it will be a lot more fun, and you'll need the support!

CHAPTER 1 SUMMARY

- Inclusion is the term used to describe the education of students with disabilities in the general education classroom with appropriate supports and services to enable them to succeed.
- Inclusion challenges at the secondary level include increased student diversity, high-stakes testing, increased content area instruction, and highly qualified teacher requirements.
- Teachers need to be equipped with a repertoire of strategies to support diverse learners in the inclusive classroom.
- Adolescents seek independence, socialization, and social acceptance. They are curious, adventurous, sensitive, vulnerable, and emotional.
- Common characteristics of adolescents included in the secondary classroom are academic deficits, cognitive deficits, social interaction deficits, organizational deficits, and motivational problems.
- Active learning is the intentional engagement of students in the learning process, supporting behavioral and cognitive objectives as well as appropriate state standards. Students are engaged, having fun, and at the same time, are at the center of their own learning experiences.
- Adolescent learners prefer active learning strategies and respond to explicit modeling, practice, organization, and structure. Adolescents respond to cooperative and social learning experiences.
- Legislation, such as IDEA and NCLB, continues to increase the number of students in the inclusive classroom and requires that secondary special educators become highly qualified in content area instruction.
- Active learning strategies can support attainment of state standards and successful performance on state assessments.
- Active learning can support teachers in their efforts to differentiate instruction to improve the performance of all learners.

2

Active Learning Strategies in the Middle School and High School

Debunking the Myth

> *My daughter sat in her middle school class as her teacher asked, "Did you like it when you played games in elementary school, like Jeopardy and other learning games?" "Yes!" the class responded. "Well, this is middle school. We don't do that anymore; that is for elementary school only. We don't learn through fun and games here." The class fell silent with disappointment, and my daughter turned to her friend and whispered, "Oh yeah? My mom does it in college."*

We know that the story above is true, and we also know that it is not necessarily representative of all teachers. It can seem, however, that working active learning strategies into content-intensive middle school and high school grades can be a bit more of a challenge, especially because, in many cases, it calls on us to teach in a totally different style from the one in which we were taught.

This is an issue we discuss with our college students. When we expose our college students to active learning strategies, teach them the supporting research, and use the strategies in our own classes to convey course content, our students want to know why everyone does not teach this way. They remember back to their own high school experiences and discuss in which classes the learning was interactive and participatory and in which it was primarily teacher driven (i.e., the guide on the side as opposed to the sage on the stage). They talk about what they learned, what content they remembered, and what has been long forgotten. They talk about how they learn best in college and particularly about when and how they have been able to make applications that increase learning.

From all of these discussions, our takeaway is that there are still some very real concerns about how active learning plays out in the classroom and how it works from the teacher's perspective. In this chapter, we address the questions we have been asked and the ones we are pretty sure people would have liked to ask. If you find yourself asking a similar question, here are your answers.

FREQUENTLY ASKED QUESTIONS

Sounds good, but doesn't it take too much time to plan?

Not necessarily. It is more a matter of looking at lesson planning as two parts: content and process, what you will teach and how the students learn the material. Once you have set what you need to teach, you can decide which strategy best meets your needs.

Some strategies do take more time than others to set up, while others take minimal preparation once the content is in place.

The more you use active learning strategies, and the more comfortable you become, the easier it is to choose a strategy and teach with little additional time needed. The other point to consider when using active learning strategies is that, once the planning is completed, you take the role of facilitator, and the lesson flows.

Is active learning one more thing I have to do?

No. Developing active learning strategies to support content-based instruction is not an additional task. Active learning enhances and supports instruction that assists students in the learning process. Planning active learning strategies is your lesson planning and can easily be designed to meet academic objectives and state standards.

I am not creative—where should I even begin?

You already have started simply by reading this book. Look to your resources, fellow teachers, websites, and teacher magazines. Start dialogues with your colleagues, and share ideas and experiences.

Once you are comfortable with a given strategy, it is easy enough to vary it to different content. Once you have used a variety of strategies, you have a number of ideas to choose from, and you can adapt, adjust, or modify a given strategy to meet your own needs without having to come up with something brand-new.

I do want my students to enjoy learning, but will I be able to cover the content? After all, I only see my students one period a day (or for a block every other day), and if I add strategies, I may not have enough time to cover all of the content in my curriculum.

This is a common concern, particularly for middle and high school teachers. The answer goes back to the purpose of active learning, and that is to facilitate learning. A strategy should be used to help students to learn, understand, and apply content to specific learning objectives. Content is taught using the strategy—the strategy is not a fun add-on.

Some strategies lend themselves to covering new content, and others are better suited to content application or review. Some strategies are designed to enhance a lecture presentation. You may choose to vary your teaching style and intersperse active learning with direct instruction, or lecture, to impart new information. Choose your strategies wisely to match content with your objectives and student needs, and they will enhance instruction rather than take time away from it.

Student motivation is another key issue here. When students are engaged, involved, and interested in the lesson, they learn more, remember what they learn, and are more readily able to apply new information. Active learning strategies enhance the learning of content.

This kind of teaching takes too long.

Some strategies are longer than others, but consider that they are the lesson, or a portion of the lesson, as opposed to something to do in addition to teaching the lesson.

This makes sense for younger children, but this is middle school (or high school). Aren't they just supposed to sit in their seats and learn what they are taught? (OK—you are thinking that this is an old-school question, but understand that change sometimes takes a while, and sometimes we tend to teach in ways that we are more familiar with.)

Research tells us that all people learn best when they are involved in their own learning. (Chapter 1 explains this in detail.) And remember back to your own high school or college classes, or think about how you learn as an adult as you construct your own answer to this question.

What if the class gets out of control?

A reasonable concern. As with any lesson, you will need to set up expectations ahead of time. Briefly explain the rules. Use preventative behavior management as necessary. Explain the relevancy of the lesson. If something you try is clearly not working, feel free to calmly change directions and do something else, and try the strategy again at another time. Typically, students prefer more engaging lessons to sitting at their desks and working quietly, and they will stay on task.

What will the principal think if she walks into my classroom and we are all standing in a circle or if students are in groups and talking? What if, when she walks in, it takes a minute for her to actually spot the teacher in the room because

I am crouching down with a group in the back and not standing front and center in the classroom?

Communication is the key here. Explain to the principal, before the school year starts, what active learning strategies are and why you are using them. Clearly delineate lesson objectives. Invite her into your classroom to observe (or even better, to participate). Invite questions. Share research (including Chapter 1 in this book) that describes the benefits of active learning strategies and why this fits with what we know about how children and adolescents learn.

Consider offering to turnkey what you have learned and run an inservice, present at a workshop, or facilitate a discussion or study group for the teachers at your school. This book, for example, can serve as the basis for an ongoing study group delving into using active learning strategies.

What if my students go home and tell parents that they "played a game in math class today," in answer to the inevitable question of, "What did you do in school today?"

Create opportunities to introduce active learning to students and families.

At back-to-school night, in a letter home, or on your class website, describe your teaching style, and tell parents about some of the things you will be doing in class. Consider modeling a quick strategy at a meeting. Suggest parents question their children further (What did you learn that you did not know? How can you use what you learned?).

The other piece of this is that, in class, be clear about what the learning objectives are for the day. Use closure as an opportunity for students to reflect on what they learned during a lesson.

What do I do if a strategy does not work?

Do the same thing you do after every lesson you teach—reflect, evaluate, reassess student needs, plan, and implement accordingly for the future.

Some of my students are reticent to participate in class.

Start with strategies that are closer to previous learning experiences students have already had. Choose strategies in which less individual risk taking is expected. To start out with, choose a strategy that includes more than one learning style so that students can choose to complete the task using their favored modality. (Adolescents appreciate choice.)

More complex strategies might be most effective when you use them the first few times with familiar content (i.e., movies, sports, something students know well and have an interest in) rather than with new and difficult material.

Explain to students the purpose and benefits of active learning strategies.

For students with specific learning needs, you may support participation by introducing and practicing a given strategy ahead of time before the day of instruction.

REFLECT ON THE EXPERIENCE

- Did the students have the prior knowledge or skills they needed?
- Did the students understand what they were supposed to do?
- In retrospect, did the content not fit with this particular strategy? Would another strategy have been more effective with this content?
- Was there something else going on with the class at the time?

DURING THE LESSON

- Change it up as needed (teachers ace flexibility on the spot).
- Emphasize lesson objectives, so it is clear that learning is the goal.
- If all else fails, calmly and quietly punt and continue the lesson in a more traditional way.

AFTER THE LESSON

- Reflect on this experience, and decide if you want to try this strategy another time, another way, or with different content.
- Is there something you can fine-tune, readjust, or change so it is potentially more successful?
- Discuss your experience with a colleague; input is always valuable (and commiserating helps too!).

FINAL THOUGHTS

If you are new to using active learning strategies as a teaching tool or new to working with the adolescent population, we understand that you may have some concerns. Any new undertaking has the potential to be daunting. We trust that this chapter was able to address some of your potential concerns. It was based on many conversations we have had with preservice teachers as well as teachers in the field.

And whether you are new to active learning strategies or have been using them for years, we wish you and your students a productive learning adventure.

3

Selecting and Implementing Active Learning Strategies for the Inclusive Classroom

It is crucial to know the purpose of the lesson for which you are choosing a strategy and to keep the lesson objective(s) in the forefront when choosing the strategy, planning and implementing the lesson, and developing the assessment. Equally important is to know your students and how they learn best. This chapter is designed to help you choose, use, and reflect on active learning strategies to maximize learning and understanding in your inclusion classroom.

CLASSIFICATIONS AND CHARACTERISTICS

IDEA is the federal legislation that defines classifications for students with disabilities. These classifications help to identify students who are entitled to special education support and services in public school. Classifications are determined by a team of evaluation experts using a student study multidisciplinary team approach and are accepted by parents before identification and placement. Students with disability classifications will be part of the inclusion classroom. IDEA classifications for students with disabilities are described in Figure 3.1.

Figure 3.1 Disability Classification Chart

Autism: A developmental disability significantly affecting verbal and nonverbal communication and social interaction, generally evident before age three, that adversely affects a student's educational performance. Other characteristics often associated with autism are engaging in repetitive activities and stereotyped movements, resistance to environmental change or change in daily routines, and unusual responses to sensory experiences. The term *autism* does not apply if the student's educational performance is adversely affected primarily because the student has an emotional disturbance, as defined below. A student who shows the characteristics of autism after age three could be diagnosed as having autism if the criteria above are satisfied.

Deaf-Blindness: Concomitant hearing and visual impairments, the combination of which causes such severe communication and other developmental and educational needs that the student cannot be accommodated in special education programs solely for students with deafness or students with blindness.

Deafness: A hearing impairment so severe that a student is impaired in processing linguistic information through hearing, with or without amplification, and that adversely affects a student's educational performance.

Developmental Delay: For children from birth to age three (under IDEA Part C) and children from ages three through nine (under IDEA Part B), the term *developmental delay,* as defined by each state, means a delay in one or more of the following areas: physical development, cognitive development, communication, social or emotional development, or adaptive (behavioral) development.

Emotional Disturbance: A condition exhibiting one or more of the following characteristics over a long period of time and to a marked degree that adversely affects a student's educational performance:

(a) An inability to learn that cannot be explained by intellectual, sensory, or health factors.
(b) An inability to build or maintain satisfactory interpersonal relationships with peers and teachers.
(c) Inappropriate types of behavior or feelings under normal circumstances.
(d) A general pervasive mood of unhappiness or depression.
(e) A tendency to develop physical symptoms or fears associated with personal or school problems.

The term includes schizophrenia. The term does not apply to students who are socially maladjusted, unless it is determined that they have an emotional disturbance.

Hearing Impairment: An impairment in hearing, whether permanent or fluctuating, that adversely affects a student's educational performance but is not included under the definition of *deafness.*

Intellectual Disability, formerly Mental Retardation: Significantly subaverage general intellectual functioning, existing concurrently (at the same time) with deficits in adaptive behavior and manifested during the developmental period, that adversely affects a student's educational performance.

Multiple Disabilities: Concomitant (simultaneous) impairments, the combination of which causes such severe educational needs that they cannot be accommodated in a special education program solely for one of the impairments. The term does not include deaf-blindness.

Orthopedic Impairment: A severe orthopedic impairment that adversely affects a student's educational performance. The term includes impairments caused by a congenital anomaly, impairments caused by disease (e.g., poliomyelitis, bone tuberculosis), and impairments from other causes (e.g., cerebral palsy, amputations, and fractures or burns that cause contractures).

Figure 3.1 (Continued)

Other Health Impairment: Having limited strength, vitality, or alertness, including a heightened alertness to environmental stimuli, that results in limited alertness with respect to the educational environment, that

(a) is due to chronic or acute health problems such as asthma, attention deficit disorder, or attention deficit hyperactivity disorder, diabetes, epilepsy, a heart condition, hemophilia, lead poisoning, leukemia, nephritis, rheumatic fever, sickle cell anemia, and Tourette's syndrome; and
(b) adversely affects a student's educational performance.

Specific Learning Disability: A disorder in one or more of the basic psychological processes involved in understanding or in using language, spoken or written, that may manifest itself in the imperfect ability to listen, think, speak, read, write, spell, or to do mathematical calculations. The term includes conditions such as perceptual disabilities, brain injury, minimal brain dysfunction, dyslexia, and developmental aphasia. The term does not include learning problems that are primarily the result of visual, hearing, or motor disabilities; of mental retardation; of emotional disturbance; or of environmental, cultural, or economic disadvantage.

Speech or Language Impairment: A communication disorder such as stuttering, impaired articulation, a language impairment, or a voice impairment that adversely affects a student's educational performance.

Traumatic Brain Injury: An acquired injury to the brain caused by an external physical force, resulting in total or partial functional disability or psychosocial impairment, or both, that adversely affects a student's educational performance. The term applies to open or closed head injuries resulting in impairments in one or more areas, such as cognition; language; memory; attention; reasoning; abstract thinking; judgment; problem-solving; sensory, perceptual, and motor abilities; psychosocial behavior; physical functions; information processing; and speech. The term does not apply to brain injuries that are congenital or degenerative or to brain injuries induced by birth trauma.

Visual Impairment Including Blindness: An impairment in vision that, even with correction, adversely affects a student's educational performance. The term includes both partial sight and blindness.

Source: National Dissemination Center for Children With Disabilities (NICHCY), 2012. Used with permission.

OTHER DIVERSE POPULATIONS

Diverse student populations that are found among typically functioning students include culturally and linguistically diverse students, at-risk students, and gifted and talented students. *Culturally and linguistically diverse students* may have customs, traditions, and values that set them apart from their peers and interfere with their self-esteem and ability to participate in the learning experience. Some may be fluent in English, but others may be English Language Learners. Students who are linguistically diverse have the potential to develop communication problems (Lewis & Doorlag, 2006). These students come from all racial, ethnic, and socioeconomic groups. They are most often placed in general education classes; they may need additional help, and they often benefit from the same modifications that are made for students who are classified with higher-incidence disabilities (Mastropieri & Scruggs, 2000).

At-risk students are those whose current performance and future welfare are threatened by a host of complex societal issues including poverty; substance, physical, or emotional abuse; and homelessness. These students come to school with additional educational needs and require assistance so they don't become part of a school failure statistic (Lewis & Doorlag, 2006). Depending on the nature of the at-risk adolescent, some may have limited experience learning characteristics.

Gifted and talented students are those who learn more quickly than their peers and have high aptitudes. They excel in all academic areas. Some gifted students are more creative and have special talent in art or music. Opportunities for them to express themselves should be provided in the inclusion classroom (Lewis & Doorlag, 2006).

Typically developing learners, often referred to as *average*, are general education students who have no classifications for disabilities and are not considered diverse because of culture, language, aptitude, talent, or social problems. These students comprise at least 50% of inclusion classroom populations. They typically function academically and emotionally at the appropriate age and grade levels (Kame'enui, Carnine, Dixon, Simmons, & Coyne, 2002). Although they have no label or classification, certainly average learners are individuals with specific learning characteristics who will benefit from active learning strategies that suit their individual academic, social, and personal needs.

ASSESSING STUDENTS AND IDENTIFYING LEARNING CHARACTERISTICS

It is important for teachers to understand disability classifications and determine which learning characteristics each student possesses. Learning characteristics describe how a student learns and include his or her abilities, needs, dispositions, and preferences, such as learning styles and teaching modalities. Although diverse students are often labeled and described with a variety of terms, they have different individual learning characteristics that determine how they process and retain information. Some learning characteristics apply to all students, with and without classifications. Students' learning characteristics influence the choices teachers make to present, reinforce, connect, build, and reflect on the active learning process.

Students with disabilities have individual education plans that identify strengths, needs, and strategies. For all students, teachers may use a number of other assessment tools, such as learning style inventories, multiple intelligence surveys, interest surveys and interviews, observations, anecdotal records, error and task analyses, and so on. The important message is that teachers need to know their students. Teachers often feel overloaded and overwhelmed by teaching constrictions. They are told they need to teach to standards, curriculum, state regulations, district initiatives, and so on, but their priority is to teach to their *students.*

Knowing the students is critical when designing instruction. The strategies provided in Chapter 5 allow teachers the freedom to select active learning experiences that meet the needs of the different learners in the inclusion classroom. The focus here is not just students with disability classifications; the focus is on all students in the class, who they are as learners, and what they bring to the learning process. The questions teachers should ask include the following: (1) How does each of my students learn as an individual? (2) How does the class learn as a group? (3) What does each student bring to the learning process? (4) What can I provide for the learning process to be successful?

USING STRATEGIES: BEFORE, DURING, AND AFTER

Figure 3.2 is designed to help you to operationalize the active learning process. We imagine the reader saying, "OK, I am with you so far. Now what?" The charts that follow provide guidance in the following areas:

- selecting a strategy that is appropriate for the content of a specific lesson;
- selecting a strategy to meet individual student needs;
- guiding the implementation process; and
- reflecting, which includes questions to consider after using the strategy.

Figure 3.2 Disability Classification Chart

Considerations When Choosing a Strategy

When you are choosing a strategy, ask yourself the following questions:

- What are my specific academic objectives for this lesson?
- How does the strategy address appropriate state standards?
- Is the strategy a good fit with these objectives?
- If there are academic prerequisite skills students need to be successful with this strategy, do my students have the skills at this time?
- Do I have affective/social skill objectives for this lesson (e.g., working in groups)?
- Are there specific affective/social skills that students need in order to be successful with this strategy (e.g., working in groups), and if so, do they have these skills currently?
- What are the strengths and limitations of my diverse learners, and which strategies tend to accentuate those strengths?
- Does this strategy mirror the strengths of the class, as opposed to its weaknesses?
- What physical space do I need for this to work (e.g., the classroom space can be used as is; the classroom can be used if desks are pushed back; the hallway is available; the playground is off limits)?
- What materials do I need, and are they readily available or do I have to collect them and bring them to school? Can I use this strategy today or only after I have brought in the materials I need?
- Is this a strategy I can implement easily, or do I need time to prepare?
- Does this strategy fit with my needs, strengths, and comfort level?

HOW TO CHOOSE A STRATEGY TO MEET INDIVIDUAL STUDENT NEEDS

All the strategies we offer are designed to engage and motivate students and to facilitate and encourage learning. Although these strategies were developed for use with a variety of different learners and have a variety of applications, some strategies do address specific learning needs more directly than others. Consequently, they are summarized in Figure 3.3.

Figure 3.3 Strategies That Address Specific Learner Characteristics

Strategies	Learner Characteristics									
	Metacognitive Issues	Auditory Processing Concerns	Memory Issues	Low Experiential Base	Attention Needs	Higher Aptitude Learners	Interpersonal Preferences	Language Needs	Social Interaction Needs	Visual Processing Concerns
Artifact Reveal		*		*	*	*	Individual or small group	*		*
Ball Toss			*		*		Whole group			*
Barometer	*			*	*		Whole group			*
Board Quiz		*				*	Small and Whole group			*
Body Language	*	*	*	*	*		Whole or small group	*		*
Building an Experience		*	*	*	*	*	Whole group, small group, or individual	*		*
Bulletin Blog		*		*		*	Individual	*	*	
Concept Clarification	*		*	*	*	*	Whole group	*		
Exit Cards	*	*	*				Individual	*		
Face Place	*	*					Individual or small		*	*
Framework	*		*				Individual or small group			
Information RIngs		*	*				Individual	*		
Invention Convention		*		*	*	*	Individual or small group	*		*

Strategies	Learner Characteristics									
	Metacognitive Issues	Auditory Processing Concerns	Memory Issues	Low Experiential Base	Attention Needs	Higher Aptitude Learners	Interpersonal Preferences	Language Needs	Social Interaction Needs	Visual Processing Concerns
Jigsaw			*		*		Small and whole group		*	*
Linked-In	*	*			*		Whole group		*	
Listening Teams	*	*	*		*	*	Whole group with small group support			*
Next			*		*		Individual or small group			*
Philosophical Chairs	*		*		*		Whole group		*	*
Photo Finish		*	*		*		Small group	*		
Playlist					*	*	Small and whole group	*		*
Puzzle Pieces		*	*		*		Whole group or small group	*	*	
Reading Discussion Cards			*		*		Small group			*
Research Scavengers	*			*	*	*	Small group			
Round Robin	*				*	*	Small group			
Self-Reporting	*					*	Individual or whole group with small group support	*		
Spiderweb			*		*		Whole group			*
Teacher–Teacher	*			*		*	Pairs		*	*

(Continued)

Figure 3.3 (Continued)

Strategies	Learner Characteristics									
	Metacognitive Issues	Auditory Processing Concerns	Memory Issues	Low Experiential Base	Attention Needs	Higher Aptitude Learners	Interpersonal Preferences	Language Needs	Social Interaction Needs	Visual Processing Concerns
Text Message	*	*			*	*	Individual and pair	*		
Theme Boards	*	*	*		*	*	Small group			
Through Our Own Lens	*		*	*	*	*	Small or whole group			
Traveling Teams	*		*	*	*	*	Pair and small group		*	*
True or False	*						Individual and small group			*
Wanted Poster	*	*			*		Individual or small group			
We Interview	*			*	*	*	Individual, pair, or whole group	*	*	*
What Would They Say?				*		*	Small group or individual	*		*
The Whip		*			*		Whole group		*	*
Why and Because	*	*	*			*	Individual			*
Word by Word	*		*			*	Small and whole group	*		
Word Cloud		*	*		*	*	Whole or small group	*		
Zip-It	*	*	*		*		Small group	*		
Closure	*	*	*		*	*	Whole group			*

We have chosen to focus on learning characteristics because they provide information about what makes each of us unique in terms of how we learn. In addition, learning characteristics cut across disability categories. A student can have difficulties focusing because of one or more disabilities, or because he or she is distracted due to home issues, or just because he or she needs some help with staying focused.

LEARNER CHARACTERISTICS DESCRIBED

Metacognitive Issues

Metacognition is defined as "awareness and understanding of one's thinking and cognitive processes; thinking about thinking" (*Merriam-Webster Online*, 2010). Metacognition "emphasizes self-awareness of how one approaches a task in order to plan and monitor progress" (Sliva, 2004). Students who are more proficient at metacognition are more successful at attempting and completing new learning tasks (Sliva, 2004). Strategies that emphasize process and enable the learner to create and explain a concrete plan, such as Concept Clarification and Framework, support these students.

Metacognition strategies are also used to provide feedback on one's own learning. Examples of such metacognitive strategies are making predictions, checking progress, and monitoring work (Lenz & Deshler, 2004). Self-reporting is a strategy that can help an individual achieve these goals. Self-regulation, or adjusting one's own performance, is also a component of metacognition (Hallahan & Kauffman, 2006). A student with a low-incidence disability may have difficulty self-regulating, and so may a student with social immaturity or other needs. Again, strategies that support planning and evaluating help students monitor their own behavior and organize and process ideas.

Auditory Processing Concerns

"Auditory processing refers to an individual's ability to analyze, interpret, and process information obtained through the ear. It does not apply to what is received by the eardrum or to deafness, or being hard of hearing" (Sliva, 2004, p. 19).

Students with perceptual-auditory concerns can have problems discriminating sounds. They may have difficulty determining the difference between words with similar sounds, such as *fix* and *fit*. Fine and gross motor skills can be affected when tasks involve motor and visual or verbal skills simultaneously. Strategies that pair auditory and visual stimuli support learners who have difficulties with auditory processing (e.g., Face Place).

Memory Issues

Students with memory deficits typically have difficulty remembering information. Such students may experience the following:

- understand new information in class but be uncertain how to proceed once they leave class,

- have difficulty placing information in short-term memory and then have problems later retrieving it from long-term memory,
- not easily retrieve needed information from long-term memory. (Sliva, 2004, p. 20)

As explained in Chapter 2, brain-based information processing research tells us that the way in which new information is stored affects how easily and quickly it can be retrieved when needed (i.e., the "I have it on the tip of my tongue" phenomenon). Therefore, new ideas and information need to be connected to prior knowledge in order to facilitate information retrieval. An example of a strategy that helps students create connections and build memory is Traveling Teams. Strategies that include chunking, review, rehearsal, and reinforcement support learners with memory issues (e.g., Puzzle Pieces and Closure).

Low Experiential Base

Low experiential base refers to students who, for a variety of reasons, have not been exposed to many of the life experiences that most students of the same age or grade level have. They may be culturally diverse or at risk. Vocabulary is likely to be impacted. These students may not be able to relate to a story, for example, not because of lack of ability but because of a lack of experience or exposure to key elements or concepts in the story. Strategies that provide exposure to new ideas and vocabulary support these students (e.g., Through Our Own Lens).

Attention Needs

Attention affects how well students are able to maintain their concentration on a topic (Sliva, 2004). Movement and novelty often interest and motivate students with attention issues (Kounin, 1977). Active learning strategies can engage the learner who has difficulty with attention and hyperactivity by providing movement and kinesthetic activities and presenting information and learning activities in brief intervals (e.g., Body Language and Traveling Teams).

Higher-Aptitude Learners

The higher-aptitude learners are the students who need additional academic challenges. Students who can be described as *gifted and talented* fall under this category. Students with other classifications, such as behavioral issues, can also have high aptitude. They benefit from lessons that include multiple entry points (e.g., Text Message), such as working with the same content at different levels of Bloom's Taxonomy or using different sets of resources (Heacox, 2002).

Interpersonal Preferences

Some students prefer working alone, while others prefer working collaboratively. Some adolescents have distinct preferences in terms of who they work with. It is suggested that the teacher use a variety of strategies throughout the school year that provide opportunities for both. Many grouping suggestions are found in Chapter 4. During the course of the week, some lessons require students to work with the whole group; other lessons focus on small group work, cooperative learning, pairs, or working individually. Keep in mind that some of the active learning strategies can be adapted to meet different interpersonal preferences. For example, Playlist can be an individual or cooperative experience.

Language Needs

There are students who are English Language Learners. They have difficulty with expressive language, which impacts their abilities to explain things verbally or complete tasks such as rapid oral drills. There are students who have difficulty with receptive language; this type of learner has difficulty connecting vocabulary words to their meanings (Sliva, 2004). Students who have one or more of these language issues may need additional time or prompts to answer questions, practice with vocabulary words, or the opportunity to demonstrate an answer rather than explain it verbally (e.g., The Whip). Visual or concrete props in a strategy support extemporaneous speech (e.g., Invention Convention).

Social Interaction Needs

The adolescent learner craves social experiences and social acceptance. Strategies that support social interaction and create positive social experiences strongly support and motivate this population.

Students with poor or limited social interaction have difficulty engaging appropriately with their peers. They seem less mature or reticent and may have low self-esteem. They have trouble reading social cues and misinterpret the feelings and emotions of others, often responding inappropriately (Hallahan & Kauffman, 2006; Mastropieri & Scruggs, 2000). They can be ignored and left out or ridiculed by others. They may not understand when they are bothering others, and they may not know how to view things from another person's perspective. Strategies that promote role-play or group interaction or specific turn-taking directions and peer support, such as Linked-In or Puzzle Pieces, can support individuals with social skill issues.

Visual Processing Concerns

"Students with visual-processing difficulties have trouble making sense of information visually. Some implications of these difficulties include losing their place on a page or worksheet or while reading a text; confusing unrelated information on a page; reversing letters or digits; and the inability to differentiate objects based on their individual characteristics" (Sliva, 2004, p. 28).

For example, students with visual processing issues may have trouble solving puzzles and remembering shapes (Hallahan & Kauffman, 2006). Strategies that use multimodalities and multisensory approaches, pairing visual stimuli with other modalities, enhance learning for these students, such as Invention Convention. Discussion also supports the learning experience for students with visual processing concerns. Strategies such as Artifact Reveal or Invention Convention support these students.

Learner Considerations

We know that all people have both strengths and weaknesses in terms of how they learn best. If we identify the weakness and avoid them in order to encourage success, then we run the risk of weakening this learning modality even further. The idea is to teach to the strengths and remediate the weaknesses.

Figure 3.3 suggests which strategies may give students the chance to practice and strengthen specific learning characteristics that may be affecting the way they comprehend new material.

HOW TO CHOOSE A STRATEGY TO MEET INDIVIDUAL TEACHER NEEDS

The purpose of this book is to empower you as the teacher in the classroom. Take into account your own strengths, needs, preferences, and skills when you choose strategies. Although it is important to design lessons to support how adolescents learn, it is also important to consider yourself as well. Who are you as a teacher? What is your comfort level with movement and transition?

Consider your teaching style. How can you best facilitate your class? Would you benefit from trying something new? Be sure you are comfortable with the complexity of the strategy before using it. Practice strategy implementation before introducing it to the class. Although we recommend new ideas, teacher motivation and enthusiasm certainly impact the success of the student learning experience. Figure 3.3 helps you consider which strategies may be most useful for you and your class and determine whether the strategies were successful.

LEARNING COMMUNITIES

In many schools, teachers are forming learning communities to continue to study teaching and learning. The questions posed in this chapter lend themselves to discussion, whether in a formal leaning community with set hours and agendas or in informal discussions with the ninth grade team, with the student study team members you work with, or with the people you eat lunch and share your successes and frustrations with. Often in inclusion classrooms, two teachers work together to maximize learning. The questions in Figures 3.4, 3.5, and 3.6 are designed to open a meaningful dialogue on planning for instruction in any and all of these situations.

AND NOW, THE NEXT STEP OF OUR JOURNEY

We have worked our way through the reasons why active learning is so important and the nitty-gritty on how to choose and apply the strategies. Stick with us as we discuss why and how to use grouping for instruction in the inclusion classroom and then describe the strategies.

CHAPTER 3 SUMMARY

- Students who receive special education services must have one of the IDEA classifications: autism, communication disorder, deaf-blindness, hearing impairment, cognitive impairment, multiple disabilities, orthopedic impairments, other health impairment, emotional disturbance, traumatic brain injury, or visual impairments.
- Diverse groups among typically developing students include culturally and linguistically diverse students, at-risk students, average learners, and the gifted and talented.
- All these students, with and without classification, can benefit from active learning strategies in the inclusive classroom. In order to identify which strategies support specific learners, look at the students' individual learning characteristics. A description of each of these characteristics and the types of strategies that support these needs are included in this chapter. Learner characteristics include metacognitive issues, auditory processing concerns, memory issues, low experiential base, attention needs, higher-aptitude learners, language needs, social interaction needs, and visual processing concerns.
- The Strategies That Address Specific Learner Characteristics chart (Figure 3.3) identifies the 41 active learning strategies and their corresponding learner characteristics.
- Teacher Notes and Reflections, Figure 3.6, helps the teacher consider strategy selection and implementation for specific student needs and then reflect on the lesson.

Figure 3.4 Considerations for Implementing a Strategy

Considerations for Implementing a Strategy

- Make a direct connection between the strategy and what you want students to learn.

- Establish the purpose of the lesson so that students know what the objectives are and what they will be learning. Consider your process and outcome for the lesson. This is particularly helpful for those with specific learning disabilities in order to help them to relate new content and previously learned material and to enhance short-term and long-term memory, storage, and retrieval.

- Gather or construct materials, and try them out before the lesson so you know they will work the way they should.

- Use closure to assess what the students learned, and reflect on the experience. What did you expect your students to learn? What did the students produce, connect, reflect on, or conclude?

Figure 3.5 Considerations After Using a Strategy

Considerations After Using a Strategy

- Did the students learn what I wanted them to learn?
- How do I know that the students learned what I wanted them to learn?
- Were the students able to follow the directions? Should I modify the way I give directions or how I explain what they need to do?
- Were all students motivated and engaged? Did everyone appear to be comfortable participating?
- Did this strategy enhance the experience of the classroom community and allow diverse learners to work together productively?
- What would I do differently next time?
- Could I bring in more comparisons or develop more syntheses, such as alternative perspectives and text-to-text or text-to-self connections?
- What other academic content could I use with this strategy?
- What were the benefits of using this strategy (e.g., it spurred a lively conversation about the content)?
- Were there any drawbacks to this strategy (e.g., it took more time than expected)?
- Would I recommend it to my colleagues? Why or why not?
- Would I consider using it again?
- Rate your own enthusiasm or motivation for this strategy.

Figure 3.6 Teacher Notes and Reflections

Teacher Notes and Reflections

How this connects to my philosophy of inclusion

What I want to share with colleagues

Connections to my students' learning characteristics

When I consider my students this year, what learning needs do I feel take precedence as I plan for instruction?

My "aha!" moments

My questions

4

Grouping for Instruction

Who Goes Where With Whom to Do What

Inclusion in middle school and high school has a unique set of challenges. All teachers question how they can meet the needs of all learners, but middle school and high school classrooms are content intensive. Teachers think about whether they need to take more time to teach material, and if so, will there be enough time to cover all of the material? If lessons proceed more slowly, will they lose the interest and attention of another group of learners? Will this lead to unwanted classroom behaviors? And, with inclusion, how will this affect social interaction in the classroom? Will some students be left out or not fit in? These are some of the thoughts swirling around when the word *inclusion* comes up in the secondary school community.

HOW DO I MANAGE EVERYONE?

Philosophically, the inclusion classroom is designed so that students learn together. The challenge is to meet individual learning needs in a way that keeps the group cohesive and allows the class to cover the content. There are two key issues here. The first is that, when teachers use sound educational practices, including active learning strategies, the whole class benefits. The purpose of active learning strategies is to teach, reinforce, and practice content. This is true for all age and grade levels. One of the benefits is that the strategies we discuss in this book accommodate a variety of different learning needs at one time. Active learning strategies work for all types of learners. As we tell our preservice teachers, "Good teaching is good teaching."

The second key issue is flexible grouping. Flexible grouping ensures that students are not pigeonholed with one specific group of learners, working with the very same people every lesson, every day, every week. Is it really an inclusion classroom if you group all the classified students together for every class period?

Flexible grouping enables students to work with and get to know a variety of classmates over the course of the year. "Students with special needs benefit from both whole group (or large group) and small group instruction" (Friend & Bursuck, 2009, p. 169).

Flexible grouping is an important component of inclusion and of any instruction that is differentiated, but groups should not isolate particular populations. Flexible grouping, which includes whole group instruction, small group instruction, pairs, and individual work, creates a wide range of options. Teachers can decide which type of group to use, depending on the subject area and the lesson in question, the active learning strategy, and the needs of the class.

Many of the active learning strategies in this book are designed to be used with the whole group. "The challenge in a whole-group setting of diverse learners is to avoid teaching solely in the way you were taught or the way you learn best" (Hollas, 2007, p. 16). We need to use a variety of strategies in an inclusion classroom in order to reach many different learners.

WHOLE GROUP INSTRUCTION

Sometimes, whole group instruction is your most effective teaching method. For example, you'll want to instruct the whole class when you're doing one of the following:

- building community through common activities or experiences;
- introducing new units, topics, skills, or concepts; or
- conducting discussions of important content (Heacox, 2002, p. 88).

Building a classroom community is essential for any inclusion classroom, regardless of grade level. All the students should be participating members of this community, not just physically taking up space in the same room. This is a challenge in general in middle school and high school, with all of the changes that adolescence brings along with changing routines, typically with movement from class to class.

Active learning addresses this issue. In the first place, when people work together as a class, trying something different, they have the opportunity to relate to one another in a variety of different ways. The strategies influence the classroom dynamic positively. These strategies allow different strengths and skills to emerge, providing opportunities for increased confidence in the classroom. If group members are asked to do something different, slightly out of their comfort zone, there can be the feeling of being in this together, even laughing as a group as opposed to at an individual.

Also, many of the strategies in this book have adaptations that focus specifically on community building, which provides opportunities for students to get past perceptions and outward appearances and get to know one another as individuals. This is something that is frequently not top priority in middle school and high school as it comes second after high-stakes testing and covering massive amounts of content. The strategies here are developed to advance content knowledge and to teach new material in a way that simultaneously addresses the critical need for community building. One of these areas does not have to supersede the other.

Some of the strategies allow for purposeful movement that helps the adolescent to focus on the task at hand. Class discussions, as noted, are important. Active learning strategies facilitate meaningful discussion among classmates, easily supporting reluctant participants such as the student who has an expressive language difficulty or a second language learner. These strategies may be adapted to allow for additional processing time after hearing the question or sentence starter, or they let the teacher structure the discussion so that everyone has an opportunity to talk. (We all remember those class discussions where a few people dominate, a few more work hard at getting noticed to interject their own thoughts, and the rest tune out due to lack of interest or they just choose not to participate.)

SMALL GROUP INSTRUCTION

In secondary classrooms, teachers often have students work in small groups, and these groupings can vary depending on the task at hand. Often, time is of the essence, and students get grouped quickly by who they sit next to. We offer a number of different ways to form groups to take into account the need for students to work with a variety of classmates over the course of the semester. (See Figure 3.3 in Chapter 3.)

DIFFERENT WAYS TO FORM GROUPS

As we have discussed, flexible grouping is one of the elements in a successful inclusive classroom. The strategies in Chapter 5 utilize a variety of group formats. In the remainder of this chapter, we will discuss grouping options for middle and high school classes.

GROUPING BY STRENGTHS: TWO TYPES

Group Students With Similar Strengths

This is also known as homogeneous grouping.
It is beneficial when

- You want to give each group a different level of reading material.
- The task at hand is predicated on skills the students have already acquired.

(Continued)

(Continued)

Group Students With Differing Strengths

This is also known as heterogeneous grouping.
It is beneficial when

- The task will benefit from different types of learners.
- Each group will benefit from having a leader, or a student who is good in art, and so on.
- Students can support their peers.
- Students have the opportunity to work on collaborative skills.

Grouping by Interest

Groups are formed by grouping students who choose the same topic or subject matter to work on.

What It Looks Like

- Students choose the topic they want to work on from a teacher-provided list of choices.

Benefits

- Students have the opportunity to share common interests.
- Adolescents particularly appreciate choice.

Grouping by Preference/Learning Style

Students identify their favorite learning styles and how they learn best, and the teacher uses this information to form groups.

What It Looks Like

- Students are given particular topics to research. They are given a choice of finding out information using one of the following sources, and students who are interested in similar types of research can work together:
  - Books
  - Periodicals
  - Other news sources as appropriate
  - The Internet
  - Alternate technology
  - Personal interviews
  - Museum or historical sites (this can be as a field trip, on the Internet, or through library books)
  - Architectural designs of a certain age, period, or country

Benefits

- It motivates students.
- It capitalizes on and emphasizes individual strengths rather than weaknesses.
- It can build confidence.
- It allows students to work with others with similar interests and skills or people they may not have had the opportunity to, or chosen to, work with previously.
- It gives each student the chance to be seen by others in his or her best light. (In contrast, for example, if we, the authors of this book, are always put in the technology group, we would be perennially the followers and have no chance of showing our true capabilities, but put us in the interview group, and we will both shine!)

Grouping by Student Choice

Students select who they want to work with.

What It Looks Like

- Students are told to form groups of three.

Benefits

- Adolescents are social beings and appreciate the opportunity to work with their friends.
- It is effective when it is one of several methods of grouping.

It's best to use student choice carefully as we want to encourage choice but at the same time provide an environment where no student feels excluded by peers. This is especially important for adolescents as at this stage social acceptance is critical.

Random Grouping

Student groups are formed with no particular plan as to who goes in which group.

What It Looks Like

- Students count off, and all the ones work together, all the twos, and so on, or each student is given a colored poker chip and is then directed to join the other students with the same color chip.

Benefits

- It is efficient and convenient.
- Students have the chance to work with most everyone in the class over the course of the semester.

Apparently Random Grouping

The teacher uses a grouping system that appears to the students to be random but actually is not. You have determined in advance which students you would like working together for a given strategy or assignment as well as which students would be best separated for the time being. When using any of these grouping systems, the teacher can plan to put together, or to keep apart, specific students as she or he "randomly" assigns the groups.

What It Looks Like

- Appointment book partners: Photocopy one page from an appointment book that has a space for an appointment every half an hour. Give students a few minutes to walk around the room and sign up for "appointments" with each other. The rules are these: Only sign each person's book in one place; two students sign each other's book for the same time period, so, for example, the authors of this book are signed up as each other's 2:30 p.m. appointment, and other people will have to choose appointments at different times; when the teacher wants students to be paired up, she simply asks students to move to sit with their noon appointment, for example (and you have instant pairs). As the teacher, if you want certain students to be paired up for a given lesson, look at what times they have in common, and call that time.

Modified Attribute Cards

Type of playing card **ACE**	Name of Author
Multiple of 7 **35**	Technology Source **Smart Phone**

- Set these up before school starts. You will need one large, unlined index card per student. Divide them into fourths. Decide how many groups you need. If you have 20 students and want them in pairs, make a list of 10 different types of playing cards (i.e., ace of hearts, 10 of diamonds). Two cards will have the ace of hearts, two cards will have the 10 of diamonds, and so on. To get them in pairs, ask the students to match up with people who have the same card type as they do on the index card.
- Colored dots (Avery makes pages of colored dot stickers in a variety of sizes): If you have 24 students, give 6 of them handouts, each with a red dot on it, another 6 get handouts with yellow dots, then the next 6 get handouts with

blue dots, and so on; ask students to get into groups according to the color dot on the paper, and you have four seemingly random groups ready to work. You can also keep a stack of different-colored index cards to hand out, and then ask students to get into groups with the others with the same color index card. Or run off handouts on three or four different colors of paper, and students use the colors of their handouts to sort themselves into groups.

Benefits

- It can be done on the spur of the moment once the partner sheets have been completed. Partner sheets can be completed within the first few weeks of school and glued into the cover of a folder or notebook or laminated for durability.
- It may take less time and be more inclusive than asking the students to find someone to pair up with.
- The teacher can control who is working with whom (or which pairs need to be split up) in a subtle way.
- Students have the chance to work with a variety of classmates throughout the course of the year.

Content, student characteristics, academic and behavioral needs, and lesson objectives determine which type of grouping will be most effective for a specific class's instructional needs at any given time. Varying the way students are grouped maximizes learning opportunities and keeps the inclusion philosophy in the inclusion classroom.

We have discussed the importance of flexible grouping and described a number of ways to achieve this goal. The box below contains suggestions to make the process run more smoothly.

At the beginning of the year, set out clear expectations for groupwork, and explain the importance of it. This is just as important, if not more so, at the middle school and high school level as at the elementary level. Explain to the class how working with other people effectively is an integral part of the work environment and how the importance of working collaboratively and effectively with groups of people is a skill they will need as members of the workforce.

To start this off, at the beginning of the year, consider requiring students to research jobs in which people have to work with others collaboratively, or who have to work on committees, or who spend at least part of the workweek working in teams. Alternatively, students can interview their parents and other family members, or even teachers in the school, about this issue. You can start out the second week of school with students reporting back on what they have learned. This establishes early on the importance of effective groupwork as a lifelong skill.

AND NOW (DRUM ROLL, PLEASE) . . . THE STRATEGIES

We've discussed the *what:* inclusion and active learning. We've discussed the *why:* Teachers are responsible for addressing diverse student needs in the inclusive classroom. Now, we come to the *especially how* part. Many of you may be saying, "Sure, I agree with all that, but the tough job is making it happen." We've been there and know the feeling, but we hope to alleviate that stress with Chapter 5. Enjoy, and we hope your students do too!

CHAPTER 4 SUMMARY

- Flexible grouping can be instrumental to the successful implementation of active learning strategies.
- With the focus on including students in active learning, several grouping options are available to meet student and teacher needs.
- Whole group instruction is often beneficial for community building, introducing new units and ideas, and discussing important concepts.
- Small group instruction can be arranged by like ability, mixed ability, interest, learning styles and preferences, or randomly. Each method has specific benefits.
- Tips to support appropriate group instruction and management include the following: Change groups as appropriate to meet different needs; encourage students to be supportive, patient, and positive with one another; and allow time for groups to share outcomes and meaningful feedback with each other.
- Remind students to use effective feedback. If this is likely to become an issue, have students use literature, movies, or even TV shows to come up with a list of remarks that qualify as positive feedback and a list that qualifies as negative feedback. You can do this at the beginning of the semester, or it can be ongoing; for example, as part of a discussion of literature, you can examine the interaction that key characters have with each other. (In a social studies class, you can do the same exercise by reading the newspaper, listening to politicians on TV, or observing political campaigns.)
- Capitalize on opportunities for groups to process and share what they have learned or produced with the whole class.

5

Active Learning Strategies

In Chapter 1, we explained the relevance of active learning and the way in which strategies incorporate active learning and engage the learner. We reviewed the significant role that motivation plays in student learning, and we made a case for increasing motivation to encourage learning and understanding. In Chapter 2, we explained why active learning can be an effective part of instruction in the secondary inclusive classroom.

In this chapter, we present a wide variety of strategies that promote active learning. These strategies are motivating because they include movement, interaction with peers, topics of particular interest, or different ways of rehearsing content, or they allow for student voice, divergent answers, or multiple methods of response. They are motivating because they are appealing to students and they are fun.

Each strategy provides a framework for the teacher to develop a variety of lessons that encourage and engage students; teach, reinforce, and facilitate application of content; and provide opportunities for reflection. Our strategies are presented in alphabetical order, with the exception of Closure, which appropriately resides at the end of this chapter, with information about how and why to use each strategy. We offer strategies with multiple suggestions for use, and we encourage you to use them as you see fit to benefit your learners while addressing their needs and making connections to the curricula.

STRATEGY 1

Artifact Reveal

Explanation

Students create artifacts that exemplify something they learned about. Students share artifacts and create a classroom museum, sharing concepts and commentary with one another.

Materials

- Random items or similar items in bags (Student groups get the same or different items distributed in bags. Items can include tissue paper, pipe cleaners, yarn, a magazine, and so on.)

or

- Materials students have at home to create artifacts
- Rubric
- Class commentary sheets—blank sheets of paper where students can make comments about peer projects and the topic studied

Advance Preparation

- Select learning objectives related to artifact development.
- Determine if students will work in groups, pairs, or individually.
- Decide to prepare materials for students, or allow students to select and bring in their own materials.

Directions

1. After selecting a concept or individual that is important to a learning experience, ask students to create an artifact that would be meaningful to the area of instruction being studied.

2. Allow students opportunities to work on the artifact in school or at home. Allowing students to work at least partially in school together encourages cooperative learning through brainstorming, critical thinking, and kinesthetic activities.

3. Remember that the artifact share is a classroom experience, not a science fair–scale assignment; therefore, allow no more than three days to complete artifacts.

4. Ask students to complete a simple assignment rubric:

- Artifact name and description _____/5
- Meaning/significance to topic studied _____/5
- Execution/presentation _____/5

5. On the day of the Artifact Reveal, students place artifacts and rubric information on desks. Classmates may walk around the classroom writing comments on the class commentary sheets. Guidelines for appropriate comments include positive feedback and any information that supports or relates to the concept of the artifact.
6. After the students walk around and make comments, call time. The group or pair at each artifact will share information about the artifact from the rubric and commentary sheet. The builders of the artifact can respond to any questions or make clarifications and contributions as appropriate.
7. Artifacts may remain on display or go home after the presentation.

Sample Applications

Science
- Geology terms, classifications, cell structures, and so on

Social Studies
- Information related to a historical figure, a period such as the Renaissance, or an event such as war or apartheid

English
- Novel, short stories, plays, or specific characters

Implementation Considerations

- Assigning concepts or individuals to students, you can differentiate for various student abilities and interests.
- To eliminate repetition, you may ask students to work on different parts of a concept, such as before, during, or after the Civil War.

How This Strategy Can Support Individuals With Learning Differences

- This strategy supports the adolescent as it provides structured social learning experiences.
- Even in a high-tech world, good ole making stuff still motivates and engages the young adult.
- Working in pairs or small groups reduces the chances of being embarrassed to build or present to peers.
- Students may be assigned different names or concepts based on ability.
- Visual and auditory presentations support different learning modalities.
- The products from this strategy create concrete review materials.
- Artifacts provide samples for students to share information and perspectives, supporting learners with low experiential bases or learners with language concerns.

Vignette Sample: Social Studies

In a unit on the Civil War, Mrs. G. took all the topics from her study guide and asked students to create an Artifact Reveal as a class review. The process took three days. She distributed different topics to small groups of two and three. The larger groups were assigned two artifacts, and the smaller groups were assigned one artifact each. On the first day, Mrs. G. gave out the artifact topics to the groups and allowed them to work together for 20 minutes using resources to develop rubric information and discuss artifact creation. Each group had to bring in materials and make their artifacts in class on Day 2, and they were put on display with rubric information and comment sheets.

On Day 3, Mrs. G. distributed study guides with all artifact topics to every student. Students were expected to walk around the class in their groups, reviewing and commenting on artifacts, while each student filled in his or her own study guide with information learned from the museum walk. Samples of artifact topics included the following: Confederate and Yankee industry, cotton, tobacco, clothes, causes of the Civil War, slave ships (paper boats), and a picture of a fist and coins glued to the map of the North and South to symbolize power from both parties. These artifacts were not elaborate but provided concrete visual examples to identify meaningful concepts and perceptions of the North and South in the Civil War. Mrs. G. allowed the class to walk around for two thirds of the period to view, comment, and complete study guides.

In closure, for the remaining 20 minutes of the period, Mrs. G. asked one student to explain her artifact and read one peer comment. Other students shared what they wrote on their guides. Students could agree, disagree, or embellish on study guide information with their peers. Mrs. G. found this an exciting yet simple way for students to share and review material with opportunities to use a variety of different learning modalities. This was a great way to ensure students reviewed for the exam and had study materials for home, which they created collaboratively.

STRATEGY 2

Ball Toss

Explanation

This strategy uses a ball with a variety of questions written on it as a tool for students to discuss, review, and share information and perspectives.

The Ball Toss is a classic strategy that engages students from early childhood to the university level!

Materials

- Permanent marker
- Ball (e.g., beach ball or Nerf ball)

Advance Preparation

1. Develop a list of questions. Most questions should be related to content with some humorous or personal interest questions disbursed throughout.
2. Use a marker to write questions all over the ball.
3. Once a question is written, draw a ring around it.

Directions

1. Toss the ball to a student to begin the game.
2. That student answers the question that her or his left thumb has landed on.
3. If the question has already been asked, the student chooses a question under another finger.
4. If a student has answered a question incorrectly, peers may help out.
5. The ball can only be thrown to those who have not had a turn.
6. Continue tossing the ball until everyone has had a chance or until all questions have been answered.

Variation: Cooperative Learning

1. Pair the ballplayers, and let them work cooperatively on one question.
2. Give students an opportunity to respond to or pass the question.
3. You can also create more than one ball with the same questions and set up groups to play independently, so more students have an opportunity to respond. If more than one group is using the ball, a key of questions and answers may be distributed to one member who leads the toss.

4. Cooperative teams may have their own balls with different questions posted on each ball. One possibility is to have Ball A with world language vocabulary and Ball B with world language conversation questions.
5. Each team, A and B, can practice on an area in which they feel most comfortable.

Sample Applications

English
- Questions related to literature or writing

Math
- Equations, formulas, problem-solving questions

Science and Social Studies
- Questions related to any topic

World Language
- Any questions in another language, vocabulary, or conjugation of verbs

Study Skills
- Students create possible test questions and answers. Questions and answers are submitted to you, and you write the students' questions on the ball.

Implementation Considerations

Timing
- Suggested duration is no more than 20 to 25 minutes.

Design
- Although all the questions may be academic, including questions with personal interest or humor always creates a sense of fun and community in the class (e.g., what is something you are looking forward to this summer, or who was your favorite teacher and why?).
- If questions are too long to place on the ball, place numbers on the ball that correspond to questions you may read to students as students call the numbers out.
- You may have students answer questions related to content even if someone else has already had the same question to provide additional reinforcement and review.

Tips
- Beach balls are good for ball tosses because they are inexpensive and can be deflated and saved for the future.
- Sometimes, even when you use permanent marker, the ink fades after a while, so be sure to save your questions if you plan to use the same ones again.

How This Strategy Can Support Individuals With Learning Differences

- This strategy can support reinforcement and memory with repetition of questions and answers.
- Students with visual processing needs are supported with an auditory learning experience.

Vignette Sample: Social Studies

Mr. N. taught an inclusion social studies class. Because there were several students in the class who struggled with the content area, he felt he couldn't do a lot of creative instructional work with them and typically had them read and answer questions from the text for instructional and review days. Students were well behaved following the routine, but interest and performance were at a standstill.

In order to motivate students and encourage review and reinforcement, Mr. N. introduced the Ball Toss strategy.

- *Why is Mother Jones a symbol of the labor movement?*
- *What was your greatest challenge or success in high school so far?*
- *Why do you think union workers gave the nickname* Mother *to Mary Jones?*
- *What were the demands of organized labor in the 1880s?*
- *What was the cause of the Haymarket Square Riot?*
- *Talk about the person you most admire.*
- *What methods did Frick use to break the steelworkers union at Homestead?*
- *Explain the difference between an industrial and a trade union.*
- *What is your favorite summer memory?*

Mr. N. placed students in a circle, explaining that, when the ball was thrown, the student who caught it could answer the question that landed under his or her left thumb or call a friend. The ball was passed, and students reacted positively with laughter and smiles. Two students called friends to learn the difference between unions and Frick's methods. No one was penalized for calling a friend. Learning about personal information in between, such as how one student's challenge was having his sister in a class together, also gave the class cause to chuckle. Mr. N. learned the Ball Toss was very motivating and could bring an inclusive class together collaboratively as a community as they had an opportunity to have a student-centered approach to sharing information learned. Done!

STRATEGY 3

Barometer

Explanation

Barometer incorporates some of the same elements as a debate. The purpose of this strategy is for each student to take a stand on a controversial issue the class has been studying or a situation that has many sides and to list the reasons that support their opinions. This encourages students to support their opinions with facts, to be persuasive, and at the same time, to consider other points of view. A lively discussion often follows.

Materials

- A large classroom with room to spread out (if this is not possible, just rearrange where the groups are seated)
- Paper and pencils for students to take notes

Directions

1. Choose a controversial topic that the students have been studying, one that has many sides to the same issue. Alternatively, propose a situation or a scenario, and see whether students agree or disagree with the process or the outcome. Describe one situation, or ask one open-ended question for the class to work on for the period.

2. Review the content, and ask students to consider how they feel about this particular issue or situation.

3. Ask students to take a stand on the issue and choose one of the following options:
   - strongly agree—Group 1
   - agree (or tend to agree)—Group 2
   - neutral (do not have a firm opinion one way or the other)—Group 3
   - disagree (or tend to disagree)—Group 4
   - strongly disagree—Group 5

4. Ask students to move into the group that corresponds with the opinions they hold. Groups will discuss why they hold the beliefs they do and list reasons to support their opinions.

5. If room allows, seat the groups in circles along vertical or diagonal lines in the classroom, with Group 1 at the head of the line, then Group 2, and so on, in sequential order.

6. Once groups have had the chance to talk among themselves, give each group five minutes to explain its position to the rest of the class and try to change the opinions of the other groups. Participants have to be persuasive,

listing the reasons that their opinions are good. Part of the process is for each group to be succinct and to influence classmates.

7. After each group has had a chance to present, ask students whether they have been persuaded to change their opinions. If so, they should stand up and move to another group. Follow-up discussion includes what students learned from each other, what they learned about the topic, and what effective ways to be persuasive may be.

Sample Applications

English

- Have the class read a novel; after is it completed, choose one of the following topics for Barometer:
  - Do you think the characters that the author created are realistic?
  - Do you think the novel was true to the period in which it was set?
  - Do you think a particular character's actions were ethical (or were justified)?
  - Do you think a particular character's actions were a catalyst for change?
- Should classic books be banned from schools and libraries because of language or subject matter?
- Another way to use Barometer in conjunction with reading a novel is to give students a few minutes to work on their own to decide what they think the most important theme or message is in a novel, and then have them get into groups according to theme; each group tries to persuade their classmates that their theme is the most important and clearly represented in the novel. After taking part in Barometer, students return to their seats to write persuasive essays embracing their own beliefs.

Social Studies

- Is war ever justified?
- Should driving age vary from state to state, or should there be one legal age for the whole country?
- Is there truth to the statement that history repeats itself? Why or why not?

Current Events

- Use the media to pose your own Barometer question relating to a news item that is relevant to your content area.

Science

- Immunizations—pro or con?
- Driving age as it relates to brain function—what is the age at which adolescents are biologically competent enough to be able to drive?
- Genetically modified food, or food grown with certain chemicals, or Food and Drug Administration testing of food to keep it safe for human consumption—effective or not?

Topics That Can Work for a Variety of Subject Areas

- Airport screening—good idea or not?

- Modern technological advances—have they helped or hindered our society?
- Athletes and steroids—should athletes be required to submit to drug testing to monitor steroid use?
- Drugs in the workplace—should mandatory drug testing be required as part of the process of being hired for a new job?

Implementation Considerations

Timing

- This strategy can take one or two class periods, depending on how long each class period is and how much time you choose to allot to this topic.

How This Strategy Can Support Individuals With Learning Differences

- The Barometer provides a metacognitive structure for students to think through controversial issues and to use facts to come to conclusions. You can extend this by asking students to write opinion papers or persuasive essays as a follow-up to the lesson.
- The structure of this strategy can appeal to students with attention issues because individual opinions are key, so everyone can choose the group he or she believes in, and there is a natural pacing to this strategy, which includes listening, considering, changing groups, brainstorming, listening again, and decision making.
- Some students can explain their positions better verbally than in writing, and the Barometer affords the opportunity for you to assess and monitor metacognitive skills.
- As needed, you can review rules of a fair debate before the class starts. The Barometer can provide subtle social skill support for students who need additional structure when discussing their opinions and listening to those of others.
- This strategy gives students the opportunity to listen to multiple perspectives on the same issues.
- For students with auditory processing issues or students who need additional time to participate effectively in content-intensive discussions, you might give the students a heads-up in the class period before you plan on using this strategy and suggest that they think about where they stand; this gives students who need it extra time to gather their thoughts; alternately, you can assign this as homework, as a reading assignment that gives students information and starts them thinking or as a brief writing assignment before the strategy is to be implemented in class.
- This develops public speaking skills in all areas of study. This is a skill that potentially can be a challenge to all learners, and this strategy provides practice and feedback in a less stressful environment.

Vignette Sample: Biology—DNA

Mrs. O.'s class was studying DNA. She wanted her students to understand the ramifications of the topic.

She posed the age-old nature–nurture question to her students and at first was greeted with total silence. She reviewed prior knowledge, the role of genetics in determining who we are, and the influence that the environment has on us as human beings. She asked students to think about what they had been studying, and to consider their own lives as well, and to decide whether they believed that nature or nurture had the strongest influence on who they were as individuals.

This was the third time that her class had used the Barometer, so they were familiar with the structure and quickly began to walk around, finding classmates who held similar views. Students were fairly evenly spread among neutral, tend to side with nature, and tend to side with nurture. There were only four students who held the strongly agree or strongly disagree position, and they were equally split between both camps. The wide range of beliefs sparked an interesting discussion, and students on all sides were able to offer evidence as to why their opinions were correct.

After each group had a chance to try to persuade the others, the teacher gave students a chance to stand up and change groups, and no one budged—everyone held firm to their beliefs.

Related Information and Resources

Barometer—Taking a Stand on Controversial Issues: http://www.facinghistory.org/resources/strategies/barometer-taking-a-stand.cont

STRATEGY 4

Board Quiz

Explanation

A small five- to six-question quiz is created for the entire class to work on collaboratively. The quiz is presented on the board in front of the room. Student groups respond to one question at a time, and the class as a whole discusses the final answers for each question. The class receives the same quiz score.

Materials

- Quiz

Directions

1. Create a quiz based on learning objectives.
2. Hand out the quiz to students, and place the quiz on the board in front of the class.
3. Assign one question to each group.
4. When groups are done with their answers, they place their responses on the board.
5. Beginning with Question 1, classmates read the responses from the board and decide if they agree with what was written or if they want to suggest changes.
6. Students discuss and problem solve until they are satisfied with all quiz responses on the board.
7. Determine the quiz grade based on the final written responses from the class.
8. Collect individual quiz papers with names to use as an assessment for instructional decisions.

Advance Preparation

- Create the quiz.
- Select student groups.

Sample Applications

Open-ended or problem-solving questions for any content area

Implementation Considerations

- Select groups heterogeneously or homogeneously, assigning problems accordingly.
- Direct each group to show all work related to problem solving, and their responses. Quizzes should specify that each student shows his or her work.
- If part of the class does not agree on an answer, you need to make a decision for this situation, such as majority rules, a silent paper vote, and so on. This strategy is intended to be a group learning experience where all students work together for one grade.
- Determine if students will work on problems with or without resources.

How This Strategy Can Support Individuals With Learning Differences

- Students work as a whole group, and therefore, no one is solely responsible for each answer. This can encourage reluctant learners to take risks.
- Students in groups have opportunities to learn from one another in this cooperative learning experience. No one is singled out.
- This strategy provides an opportunity for the class to work together and boost their grades in a brief assessment experience.
- This strategy supports high-aptitude learners who can be assigned more challenging questions.
- The strategy supports students with auditory and visual needs as it uses both visual and auditory presentation.

Vignette Sample: Algebra

In an algebra class, the students walked in to find Mr. M. had placed a quiz on the board in front of the room. The quiz read:

1. $X^2 + 5X + 6 = (X + 2)(X + 3)$
2. $Y = b^x$ *is equivalent to* ________________
3. $-2X + 4 = 0$ *(Solve for x)*
4. *Simplify* $(X^3)(X^4)$
5. $X + 1 > -X + 5$ *(Solve for X)*

He broke the class up into five groups, with four to five students in a group. Each group was assigned a specific problem to solve. After each group finished, they selected a representative to put their response on the board. The board then looked like this:

1. $X^2 + 5X + 6 =$ **$(X + 2)(X + 3)$** *(Group 1)*
2. $Y = b^x$ *is equivalent to* **$\log_b(y) = X$** *(Group 2)*
3. $-2X + 4 = 0$ **$X = -2$** *(Group 3)*

(Continued)

(Continued)

4. Simplify $(X^3)(X^4) = \mathbf{X^7}$ *(Group 4)*

5. $X + 1 > -X + 5 = \mathbf{X > 2}$ *(Group 5)*

One by one, Mr. M. asked the class members if they agreed with the responses recorded by their peers. Students agreed with all responses except Number 3. A member of the group was asked to come up to the board to explain. Sally volunteered to go over the process with the class. She went up to the board and explained the following steps as she wrote them:

$$\begin{aligned} -2X + 4 &= 0 \\ -2X &= -4 \\ X &= \frac{-4}{-2} \\ X &= -2 \end{aligned}$$

Mr. M. then asked the class if they agreed with Group 3's explanation. Jenna from Group 5 raised her hand and explained to Sally that two negatives multiplied make a positive, so the factors for a negative number, –4, had to be a negative and a positive. So, the answer was positive 2, not negative 2, because there was already a negative factor. The rest of the class, including Group 3, voted to accept Jenna's explanation, and Sally changed the answer on the board to X = 2. The class was then asked to vote again on accepting the Board Quiz responses. They agreed. Mr. M. then told them they got all the answers correct, and each student earned 10 points.

STRATEGY 5

Body Language

Explanation

Movement-based instruction involves using the body to represent the content you are learning about. The body movements to the common children's song "Head, Shoulders, Knees, and Toes" is a simple example of this concept. It is also illustrative of the fact that something we typically do when teaching young children (make your body into a letter of the alphabet, for example) is generally not considered as a content-intensive strategy for the higher grades.

Materials

- Just yourself and your students

Advance Preparation

- Consider what you are teaching that will lend itself to physical representation.
- Develop a movement technique to illustrate the content area you are teaching.
- Type up the directions.

Directions

1. Plan to use movement-based instruction to illustrate a particular concept that you are studying. Choose a concept that fits the criteria (something that can be depicted by movement—you might have to think outside of the box).
2. Review prior knowledge with your students, specifically asking them to verbally explain the content.
3. Describe to the class what they are going to do (go over the directions). You may want to have these printed out so that your students can easily follow along.
4. Then, as a class, act out the movements that depict the concept.
5. Discuss what you have learned.

Variation

- Let your students get themselves into small groups (three to five people), and charge each group with depicting something from the current unit of study using movement-based instruction. Then, have each group teach what they have created to the rest of the class. This can be a unique test review. (You may want to review each group's work before they teach it to the rest of the class.)

Sample Applications

English

- Students can represent the Greek chorus in The Oedipus Trilogy.
- For vocabulary, have students in groups of three or more act out the word *stunned* or *incredulous* or *enormous.*

World Language

- Students can demonstrate or act out the meaning of vocabulary words, sentences, or paragraphs.

Science

- "A cell involved in the processes of protecting the cell from bacteria while letting in various enzymes," involving a ring of students representing the cell wall with one student as the bacteria and another student as the friendly enzyme (Bender, 2002)
- Simple and complex machines
- The circulatory system

Math Concepts

- Ratio, percentage
- Geometry, including shapes, different angles, and intercepting lines
- Area, perimeter
    - Students stand in a square formation to represent perimeter (see Diagram of Perimeter); to represent area, students stand shoulder to shoulder inside the square until the entire square is filled up (see Diagram of Area). This shows the students the difference between what the perimeter looks like and what the area looks like. Ask students who are part of the perimeter to raise their hands; then ask students who are part of the area (all of them) to raise their hands.
- Radius, diameter, chord, center, and circumference of a circle
    - Half of the class stands in a circle. One person goes inside the circle to represent the center; a few others go inside the circle and form a straight line from the center to the outside of the circle, representing the radius. Then, more students add to the radius line to make it into a diameter. You can extend this by naming each part of the circle and ask students who are representing a particular part to raise their hands; then you can ask a member outside the circle to walk around the circumference to show the center, radius, and diameter.
- Diagram of Area

STUDENTSTUDENTSTUDENT
STUDENTSTUDENTSTUDENT
STUDENTSTUDENTSTUDENT
STUDENTSTUDENTSTUDENT
STUDENTSTUDENTSTUDENT

- Diagram of Perimeter

STUDENTSTUDENTSTUDENTSTUDENTSTUDENT
STUDENT STUDENT
STUDENT STUDENT
STUDENT STUDENT
STUDENT STUDENT
STUDENT STUDENT
STUDENTSTUDENTSTUDENTSTUDENTSTUDENT

Implementation Considerations

- Behavioral expectations should be shared with the class at the outset of the strategy.
- You can introduce this strategy by playing charades and asking how they are able to guess the correct answer even though no talking is allowed. Explain that nonverbal communication is aided by body language and that we can use movement to convey meaning without using words. This will help your students to remember new content.
- The adolescent does not want to be embarrassed, so students who have not participated in movement-based instruction since they were young may be skeptical at first, and you might hear a grumble or two. In this case, you might want to explain the research behind it and explain how it will help with memory. The other possibility is to just work through it, and generally, the students will get involved. Having the opportunity to stand and to move during a long class period is often appreciated, and the novelty of the strategy and the curiosity of your students may very well prevail.

How This Strategy Can Support Individuals With Learning Differences

- This strategy incorporates multiple modalities as it is both visual and kinesthetic, and the visual makes the concept concrete—something students can see, understand, and remember.
- This strategy supports learners with attention issues as they are up and moving purposefully, and the novelty of the strategy positively affects motivation and time on task.
- Students with auditory processing issues benefit from this strategy as the strategy itself becomes a visual representation of the topic—students can both see the meaning and emulate the meaning. This also holds true for students who have some hearing loss.
- Research supports movement-based instruction as a way to increase memory, retention, and understanding of new content.
- Students who have a low experiential base may benefit from this strategy as well.

Related Information and Resources

- In *Differentiating Instruction for Students With Learning Disabilities*, Corwin Press, William Bender (2002) describes movement-based instruction and the research base behind it and includes examples of how it can be used in both elementary and secondary classrooms. He concludes that "as you can see from these several illustrations, the only limit on the use of this technique in the upper grades would be the limit of the teacher's creativity" (Bender, 2002).

Vignette Sample: Spanish Class

Senorita R. was looking for a way to help her students to learn the language more easily and to remember what they learned from one class period to the next, so she could build on prior knowledge at each session instead of having to reteach at each class. She decided to incorporate movement-based instruction into her classroom after reviewing the research that explains why it is effective for learners of all ages.

She started by asking the students if they remembered the song "Head, Shoulders, Knees, and Toes" from when they were growing up. She got a few giggles and a grunt or two, but most answered in the affirmative. She proceeded to teach them the song in Spanish, and each time they said the word head, *they touched their heads, and so on. A week later, when students needed to write down the Spanish word for* knees *on a test, she noticed several students surreptitiously mouthing the words to the song, tapping heads, and shoulders, and knees, and then writing down a word.*

She was teaching a lesson in verbs, and as she taught students each new phrase, she directed the class to stand, repeat the words in Spanish, and pantomime the actions at the same time. She had students pretending to climb the stairs, put away groceries, pat themselves on the back, and brush their hair while looking in the mirror while describing the motion out loud in Spanish. She repeated the process when she taught other phrases and encouraged students to pair the phrases with the corresponding movements when they studied alone at home.

Senorita R. found this was a useful strategy to incorporate into the teaching of her language. Knowing the adolescent population as well as she did after 18 years of teaching at this level, she decided that this would work best when involving the entire class at once or asking groups of five or six students at a time to act out the words as they repeated the phrases in Spanish. Pairing movement with content facilitates memory.

STRATEGY 6

Building an Experience

Explanation

You create an experience, event, or occurrence so that students can live or experience the content in order to better facilitate understanding.

Materials

- Varies

Advance Preparation

- This depends on the particular experience you are creating. Generally, advance preparation is required, ranging from simply planning out each step to a more involved process of procuring or creating materials, writing scripts, and so on. Students can help with preparation if appropriate.

Directions

1. Think about which areas of study fit best into this particular strategy.
2. Consider your objectives—what exactly you want students to know, to understand, to interpret, and to be able to utilize and apply from the material that you are studying.
3. Devise a plan. Contemplate how best your students can fulfill your lesson objectives.
4. Read sample applications, listed below, for suggestions to get started.
5. Think outside of the box. Brainstorm with colleagues. Ask former students what they best remember about the topic in question.
6. Make or collect materials as necessary.
7. The procedure to implement this strategy is related directly to the content in question, so the directions listed here are less specific than for other strategies. Reading through the sample applications can serve to clarify this process.

Variations

- After finishing up a unit, give students the opportunity to create a related experience. Ask students to write up their ideas. You can discuss what they have created and then have the option of using one or more of their ideas the following semester.
- Have students keep journals of selected classroom experiences. At the end of each of these experiences, give students time to record the experience in

their own journals, including the purpose, what they learned, and any relevant thoughts on the subject matter.

Sample Applications

Due to the nature of this particular strategy, we offer an extended application section in lieu of a vignette.

Social Studies/English/Ethics

- Every student chooses one orange from a large bowl filled with more than enough oranges for the whole class; they spend a few minutes looking carefully at their oranges and write brief biographies for them. Then, everyone puts their oranges back in the large bowl. You stir them up, and mix them around, and then let students come back up to find the same exact orange that they started with. Ask questions (What does an orange look like? Did you have a preconceived notion about oranges? How did you find your orange? Can you connect this experience to the idea of stereotypes? What did you learn?)—this experience could be related to a study of Ellis Island, for example, and how new immigrants might be treated; it could be part of a unit on tolerance connected with any number of current topics of study.
- (This example is based on an experience developed by the Anti-Defamation League.)
- Resources such as http://www.adl.org/education/education_resources_prek.asp include useful ideas and information to explore these themes in the classroom.

English/Social Studies/World Culture/Art

- Take your students on a virtual field trip (e.g., "visit" the collections in any of the worlds' great museums).
- Students work in groups. Each group chooses one ethnic group's immigration story to research. Then, they prepare three- to five-minute, first-person presentations telling the stories of the characters they have created, integrating technology if they choose. The presentations are made to 5 to 10 students each time as groups rotate through so that all students have a chance to hear all of the presentations. Audience members fill in checklists for each presentation they watch. The lesson has all four parts of language: speaking, listening, reading, and writing.

Social Studies/English

- The Feudal System—Designing an entire class period around the feudal system, preselect groups of students to represent each level in the caste system (the kings, the nobles, the lords, the villains, and the serfs). Throughout the class period, treat students according to the levels they are at, awarding privileges and rights accordingly. (A cautionary note: Prior to using this particular example, discuss it with your administrator, and let the parents know so they can continue the dialogue at home if they so choose.) Be sure to process the experience before the end of the class period, and help students to make direct connections to your area of study.

- Famous People Party—Each student chooses one of the famous people they have studied over the course of the semester and comes to a class party dressed in character and prepared to speak about his or her life, using the voice of the character too. This can also be used in English classes, using characters from novels.
- Travel Adviser—Students work in groups to research historic sites of specific regions, countries, or states and create a virtual tour for classmates; this can be effective in a European or American history course or in an English class as students create a tour of the setting in which a novel takes place.
- As part of a study of refugees, students make lists of all of the things that are important to them in real life; then, they get into groups, share lists with each other, and are given five to seven minutes to decide which things they would take with them if they had to leave in a hurry and did not know if they were coming back. The whole group has to agree, and they are allowed as many things as there are people in their group. The class uses this as a jumping-off point to discuss the concrete problems that confront refugees (adapted from Passages, an exercise prepared by Chantal Barthélémy-Ruiz, Benoît Carpier, and Nadia Clément Argine for the United Nations High Commissioner for Refugees, 1995).

Science

- As part of a study of the environment, design an experience in which everyday resources are quickly dwindling and students have to make do without resources they frequently use.
- Explain to the class that they will be working together to create the first manned space mission to Mars, using the website http://mars.jpl.nasa.gov as one of their resources (from Provenzo, Butin, & Angelini, 2008).
- Students act out the roles of villagers in a small fishing village overcome by cholera.

Math/Social Studies

- Stock Market—Students are given "school money" to invest in stocks and are required to follow their stocks throughout the course of the semester; this can be incorporated in a social studies course by relating it to the Great Depression. Students get a set amount of money, half of which is theirs to keep, but the other half they bought "on margin" borrowing through a broker. They develop portfolios, watch them, record results, and read articles pertaining to the companies. Then, you call in the loans, and they have to sell to pay back their loans.

English/Research/Writing

- Students receive $25,000 of pretend money to buy a car, but they must use Consumer Reports and investigate three different cars. They must convince you that they have made good choices. This can be part of persuasive writing or persuasive speaking; findings can be presented through an essay, PowerPoint slide show, speech, or poster.

Implementation Considerations

- Some topics lend themselves particularly well to this strategy.
- In some instances, you will explain to the students exactly what you are doing and what your intentions are for that particular lesson. At other times, students will take part in the experience without necessarily knowing what the purpose might be, and then the class can process out, discussing what they learned and how it connects to the topic at hand.
- This strategy can be as simple or as complex as the content and your imagination. It can take just a few minutes, the entire class period, or even longer as needed and as time allows.

How This Strategy Can Support Individuals With Learning Differences

- This strategy provides opportunities to intensify the understanding of particular topics and to connect them to real-world experiences that students can relate to. The idea is to make content meaningful, even for students who have not had prior knowledge of or experience with the content.
- This strategy may take students a bit out of their comfort zones, providing new experiences and making it acceptable for them to take reasonable risks (i.e., asking questions, answering more difficult questions, venturing different opinions, etc.).
- This strategy provides exposure to content vocabulary and practice with said vocabulary in applied settings and is particularly beneficial for English Language Learners and students who have language or communication issues.
- This strategy provides practice and support for social interaction. As students take part in the experience, teachers can provide feedback, as needed, and provide structure to practice skills in applied settings. Part of the experience can include group discussions of how people act in particular sets of circumstances.

STRATEGY 7

Bulletin Blog

Explanation

Based on the concept of social media and engagement, teachers and students use the classroom bulletin board to blog information, comments, and perspectives related to learning. Questions and editorials about a topic may be presented for the class community to share related information. This is a low-tech way for students to participate in a social learning experience to enhance and encourage reflection and participation.

Note: This strategy suggests an additional use of the blog concept in instruction. It is not meant to diminish or substitute the use of the original computer blog in the learning process.

The Bulletin Blog provides an opportunity for teachers and students to

- Share individual thoughts, reflections, and desires about a common topic
- Encourage conversation and discourse
- Showcase their work
- Tell stories
- Share their opinions

Materials

- Bulletin board
- Index cards
- Sticky note pads
- Pushpins

Advance Preparation

- Prepare a bulletin board as blogging station. You can put a question or piece of work in the center. Place index cards and sticky notes close by so students may use them to comment and post as needed.
- Determine how you would like to use the blog for different purposes in your instruction (see choices above).

Directions

1. Place a question, quote, student work sample, article, personal commentary, question, and so on in the center of the Bulletin Blog.
2. Ask students to respond to the work or question highlighted in the center of the blog by writing commentary on index cards.
3. When students are done, collect the comments and tack them to the board.
4. Groups of students can take turns reading student contributions.

5. Then students can discuss and share thoughts and determine the opinions of most of the class, citing rationales and agreeing or disagreeing.
6. You may also give students an opportunity to post messages, responding to one of their peers' contributions on the Bulletin Blog.
7. You may use the student comments to facilitate classroom discussion, assess student knowledge and understanding of concepts, and make further lesson-planning decisions.

Sample Applications

English

- Commentary on all parts of literature, that is, plot, character, predictions, text-to-self connections, text-to-text connections, text-to-real-life connections, moral lessons, and so on

Math

- Responding to word problems, logic or analysis questions, and so on

Science

- Word problems or commentary on social issues, for example, global warming, pollution, stem cell research, and so on

World Language

- Any question in another language

Social Studies

- Any question related to a topic studied or current events, such as, "Who do you think is the best presidential candidate, and why?"

Implementation Considerations

- Bulletin Blog can serve a multitude of purposes. Determine what best meets your instructional needs and lesson plan design. It can be used as an introduction to a topic, a classroom discussion about a topic or concept, or an exit or closing experience.
- Consider asking students to come up with the center blog information periodically. This way, students are also creating critical-thinking opportunities, not just responding to them.
- Decide if you want student identities to be revealed or anonymous. Students can write their names on the fronts or backs of the index cards.
- You may decide to grade student contributions for depth and breadth of response. Blog contributions can be part of student participation grades.
- Blogs are timely. Think about how long you might leave a blog up until you change it.
- Because different classes may use the same room at the secondary level, different classes, even grades if appropriate, can comment on the same question or another class's responses. Different-colored index cards or sticky notes may help distinguish class remarks. It can motivate classes to compare and contrast responses.

How This Strategy Can Support Individuals With Learning Differences

- This strategy supports individual and group learning social preferences.
- This strategy provides a nonthreatening opportunity to participate and share information. Such a strategy works well with individuals with social needs and low experiential bases.

Vignette Sample: U.S. Government and Economics

Do you agree or disagree with the message in this political cartoon? Explain.

In a U.S. History class, Mr. S. placed this cartoon in the center of Bulletin Blog and asked students to respond. First, Mr. S. reviewed some of the issues presented in the cartoon, such as union unrest, the rail splitter reference, and the pressures to separate the North and South. Students were asked to comment on the message of the political cartoon. Some responses were these: "Lincoln kept trying to keep the country together, and radicals from the North and South worked to undermine him. Lincoln never wanted the Civil War; he was forced into it. The South hated the rail workers and slaves; they thought they were better than everyone else."

THE "RAIL SPLITTER" AT WORK REPAIRING THE UNION.

After some discussion, Mr. S. distributed index cards and asked students to agree or disagree with the political message of the time. When they were done with writing out their responses, students pinned them on the Bulletin Blog. Students then volunteered to share responses. Overall, the majority of the class supported Lincoln's attempt to keep the country unified. Some, though, felt that Lincoln should have taken a stronger stand with the Confederacy. Such minority comments included, "The South thought they were above immigrants and factory workers and African Americans. Lincoln should have used the scissors himself to stop the abuse of these minorities, and Lincoln should use the stick to hit the man over the head. The South was taking advantage."

When students were done reading their responses, they were asked if they would like to take sticky notes and respond to peer comments. A few students did make comments to peers on sticky notes. One student responded to one of the minority messages, saying, "Violence and war is the last resort for a president; that destroys the country even more." Another student commented, "You never know how people will react. They killed Lincoln even in peace after the war. Lincoln was smart to try to work with the South instead of antagonizing them." The Bulletin Blog stayed up for a week as students learned about the events leading to the Civil War. Mr. S. referred to the Bulletin Blog and student comments periodically, asking students if they'd changed their minds with more information or had other comments to make.

STRATEGY 8

Concept Clarification

Explanation

The class works as a whole to describe and discuss abstract concepts within a teacher-directed structure that encourages discussion and debate and is an effective way to make abstract concepts more concrete to facilitate student understanding.

Materials

- Concept chart

Advance Preparation

- Prepare concept charts, one per student, and a larger diagram for you to fill in during the lesson.

Directions

1. Consider the abstract concepts, ideas, or themes from the current novel, lesson, or unit of study. Choose one.
2. Set up the concept chart on the board, and give each student a copy. (Refer to the vignette that follows to see an example of this strategy completed.)
3. This is a whole-class strategy.
4. Tell the students that, as you are working at the board, they should be filling out the chart at their seats. Fill in the name of the concept, and ask one or more students to look up the definition using a dictionary or looking online at http://dictionary.reference.com.
5. Decide, as a class, which two or three definitions you feel are most representative of the concept, and write them on the appropriate space on the chart.
6. Tells students that you are going to explore the concept in terms of what is almost always true about it, what is sometimes true, and what is almost never true. Ask the students, given what they know about the concept, what is something that is almost always true. If students are unsure what you are looking for, go ahead and tell them one idea. When there is agreement about the first "almost always," write it in the appropriate column.
7. Continue to brainstorm ideas for what is almost always true about this particular concept, writing down each answer under the "almost always" column. Encourage discussion. The discussion is an integral component of this strategy. Have students follow along on their own charts.

8. There may be a debate about whether an answer fits into the "almost always," or the "sometimes" category, for example. Encourage students to express the reasoning behind their answers. Have discussion to reach consensus, but also allow students, on their own charts, to put answers in the categories they feel are most appropriate as long as they can substantiate their choices. This facilitates understanding, helping students to own the knowledge.
9. Continue filling in the chart systematically, starting with "almost always," going on to "sometimes," and finishing up with "almost never." Very often, an answer in one category triggers ideas to add to another category, so as you near the end of the chart, you may be going back and forth between categories.
10. When the chart has been completed, have students read each section aloud, and ask what this tells them about the concept under study. Ask students to explain the concept in their own words.
11. Now that they have an understanding of the concept, ask students to list examples and nonexamples of the concept and fill these in as indicated. If there is a question about whether something is an example or not, have them look back at what the criteria is, as established by the class, for this particular concept. Let students use the criteria to determine whether it is, or is not, an example of the concept.
12. Refer back to the completed chart throughout the course of study in which this particular concept is exemplified.

Sample Applications

English

- It can be used to discuss various themes in works of fiction, poetry, or plays, such as the following:
  - love
  - trouble
  - friendship
  - trust
  - justice
  - sympathy
  - honesty
  - pride
  - future
  - forever
- It can also be used to teach vocabulary words that are abstract in nature.

Social Studies/American History

- When studying topics in American history or world history, Concept Clarification can be used to explore the meanings of any number of abstract concepts, including the following:
  - freedom
  - democracy

- peace
- responsibility
- blame
- beliefs
- liberty
- charity
- courage
- tolerance

Affective Domain (can be incorporated into English, Health, Creative Writing, Social Studies, Humanities, and Theatre Arts)

- integrity
- trust
- friendship
- sportsmanship
- respect

Math

- infinity
- time and space

Implementation Considerations

- When you are filling out the chart, there is often a debate over, for example, if a description fits in the "almost always," or "sometimes," or "almost never" category. Students can take turns explaining their positions and then can ultimately complete their own charts in the ways that make the most sense to them. There are no absolutes when developing this chart. What it does is set in motion a dialogue about the meaning of an abstract concept in hopes of helping students reach a more clear understanding, for themselves, of what it actually means.
- This strategy frequently inspires spirited discussions.

How This Strategy Can Support Individuals With Learning Differences

- It makes abstract concepts more concrete and easier to grasp.
- The product (the finished chart) provides a visual reference that students can use to check their own understanding throughout the subsequent lesson, unit, or novel.
- The focused class discussion, while filling out the chart, is a key part of this strategy. This gives students the opportunity to hear what their classmates are thinking, which also provides a model for metacognition. The emphasis here is not on a right or wrong answer but on the reasons why a concept may have certain features.
- This can be used before a lesson, novel, or unit of study that includes complex ideas as a preteaching strategy to help a few students, or the entire class, be conversant with the themes as you begin.

Vignette Sample: Social Studies—American History

Mrs. P.'s class is studying the Vietnam War. Before she started the unit, she wanted the class to understand the concept of freedom. The class put together the following concept chart based on their discussion:

Concept Clarification

<table>
<tr><td>Concept: Freedom</td><td colspan="2">Definition
• Personal liberty as opposed to bondage or slavery
• Frankness of manner or speech
• The power to determine action without restraint</td></tr>
<tr><th>Almost Always</th><th>Sometimes</th><th>Almost Never</th></tr>
<tr><td>Is positive</td><td>Is hard to achieve</td><td>Is negative</td></tr>
<tr><td>Carries responsibility</td><td>Have to work to get it; have to earn it</td><td>Is a dictatorship</td></tr>
<tr><td>Gives you choices</td><td>Taken for granted</td><td>Is severely limiting</td></tr>
<tr><td>Lets you do what you want within certain parameters</td><td>Has boundaries</td><td>Is very confining</td></tr>
<tr><td>Should be taken seriously</td><td>Has rules</td><td></td></tr>
<tr><td>You can decide what you think is best</td><td>People feel very strongly about their own freedom</td><td></td></tr>
<tr><td></td><td>Some countries have freedoms that other countries do not have</td><td></td></tr>
<tr><td></td><td>Can sometimes be difficult</td><td></td></tr>
<tr><td colspan="3">Examples of Freedom:
• Freedom of speech (being able to say what you want to say)
• Religious freedom (being able to worship the religion of your choice)
• Voting</td></tr>
<tr><td colspan="3">Nonexamples of Freedom:
• Slavery
• Incarceration
• Religious persecution (being punished for your religious beliefs)</td></tr>
</table>

Mrs. P. asked students to keep the completed diagrams in their social studies notebooks, and in subsequent lessons, she referred back to them. On more than one occasion, she asked, "Why do you think they were fighting so hard for freedom? Refer back to your concept charts, and raise your hand when you have an answer." Other questions she raised were, "What were possible drawbacks to the freedom they wanted so badly?" "Would you have risked everything for the freedoms they wanted? Why or why not?" "What freedoms do you have that are valuable to you?" Sometimes, these questions were posed as part of a whole-class discussion; at other times, they were part of small group work; and at times, she simply asked students to record the answer in their social studies journals.

Mrs. P. felt that the use of the Concept Clarification helped the class to have a better understanding of what freedom actually meant and why the desire for freedom was a strong catalyst throughout American history. She was able to build on this understanding throughout the year.

Related Information and Resources

We were given a copy of this strategy, originally called Concept Diagram, from a fellow professor in a Teacher Education Division of the Council for Exceptional Children Conference more than 15 years ago. At the time, she got the diagram from a textbook. We have been using the strategy successfully all this time and wanted to include it for our readers, but we were unsuccessful in tracking down the origin of the concept diagram. We do, however, owe a debt of gratitude to the original creators—thanks for a great idea—and to the professor who shared it with us. We hope you have the opportunity to read our book and recognize who we are referring to. We have taken the liberty to revise and embellish it.

Concept Clarification Template

Concept		Definition
Almost Always	Sometimes	Almost Never

Examples:

Nonexamples:

STRATEGY 9

Exit Cards

Explanation

Exit Cards are used during lesson closure to provide an opportunity to assess student performance. Students are given an index card and are asked to write the response to one to three pertinent questions. They submit the cards before leaving the classroom. Exit Cards can assess student understanding of content and identify student needs in the learning process.

Materials

- Index cards

or

- Cardstock cut to the size needed

Advance Preparation

- Determine what concepts you'd like to assess at the end of a lesson.
- Develop questions related to product, process, content, application, or other lesson objectives. Include questions that ask students to reflect on the learning process and their specific needs as a student; for example,
    - What was the easiest part of today's lesson?
    - What was the most difficult part of today's lesson?
    - What did you learn today?
    - What is one question you have about today's lesson?
    - Explain how you solve for x in an equation.
    - What is one part of today's lesson that you would feel comfortable explaining to someone else?
- Write the questions on index cards, one card for each student, or provide blank cards to students and ask them to write responses to questions you pose orally or on the board.

Directions

1. Five to 10 minutes before the lesson ends, distribute an exit card to each student.

2. Ask each student to write his or her name and the date on the card and work alone to respond to the questions.

3. Tell students their responses will not be used as a test. This helps identify individual student strengths and needs and reduces any anxiety related to responding to questions honestly.

4. Ask students to submit their cards to you before leaving the classroom or moving on to the next subject.
5. Use the cards to identify student strengths and needs and to make future instructional decisions. Exit Cards can be used as a grouping tool for the following day for a continuation lesson on the same topic.

Sample Applications

All subjects—any questions related to class objectives and problem solving

Implementation Considerations

- Preprinted cards with designated spaces for names and dates save time. This is one option.
- Two to three questions are typical, with one or two related to content and one related to preference and opinion about the learning process (e.g., did a student comprehend the reading; did he or she like a learning activity).

How This Strategy Can Support Individuals With Learning Differences

- For students who have trouble with writing skills, choose the option to preprint questions on cards. Multiple-choice questions can also support both recall and critical-thinking skills for metacognitive and writing needs.

Vignette Sample: Geometry

Mrs. M. was preparing students to take the Regents examination in Sequential Math. The course of study was geometry. At the end of class, she distributed preprinted cards with the following Regent sample questions:

Student Name ______________________________

Date ______________________________

Top of Form

1. Line *k* is drawn so that it is perpendicular to two distinct planes, *P* and *R*. What must be true about planes *P* and *R*?

   [1] Planes *P* and *R* are skew.

   [2] Planes *P* and *R* are parallel.

   [3] Planes *P* and *R* are perpendicular.

   [4] Plane *P* intersects plane *R* but is not perpendicular to plane *R*.

(Continued)

(Continued)

2. The vertices of Δ ABC are A(−1,−2), B(−1,2), and C(6,0). Which conclusion can be made about the angles of Δ ABC?

   [1] m < A = m < B [3] m < ACB = 90

   [2] m < A = m < C [4] m < ABC = 60

3. What is the equation of a line that passes through the point (−3,−11) and is parallel to the line whose equation is $2x - y = 4$?

   [1] $y = 2x + 5$ [3] $y = \frac{1}{2}x + \frac{25}{2}$

   [2] $y = 2x - 5$ [4] $y = -\frac{1}{2}x - \frac{25}{2}$

Bottom of Form

The results of the Exit Cards strategy allowed the teacher to determine that students were more successful working on angles and lines than developing equations. She quickly determined grouping for the following day and could spend additional time reviewing as needed with individual students. While she liked the multiple-choice idea to save time, she wasn't sure if some students just guessed at answers. Possibly one problem with showing work might have been a better indicator of student progress.

Related Information and Resources

- http://www.saskschools.ca/curr_content/mathcatch/mainpages/assess_tools/exit_cards1.html
- http://regentsprep.org/Regents/math/geometry/PracticeTests/MCTestG1.htm

STRATEGY 10

Face Place

Explanation

In this strategy, students create "Facebook" pages for specific individuals who are important to their learning experience. Then, students share "Facebook" information with peers to explain why they would or would not "friend" another "Facebook" individual created by a peer in the class.

Materials

- Teacher-made "Facebook" template or website to download template

Advance Preparation

- Select a specific topic that students need to learn more about.
- Match individual students with names and concepts that they can explain using a "Facebook" page.
- Provide a sample for students to emulate.

Directions

1. After selecting a concept or individual that is important to the learning experience of students, assign an individual or concept to each student to create a "Facebook" page.
2. You can use a teacher-made "Facebook" template or have students access the website http://www.freetech4teachers.com/2010/08/historical-facebook-facebook-for-dead.html.
3. Students are assigned or have the opportunity to choose a figure and develop a "Facebook" page (see sample template).
4. Once students complete their "Facebook" pages, explain that the class is going to become a Face Place.
5. Each student pairs with another student, and they review each other's "Facebook" pages. Then, they decide if it would be a good idea to "friend" that person or not.
6. Students share together, explaining why they have or have not decided to "friend" one another.

Variation

- The class can be placed in groups. Each group has the same assigned names and concepts. When each group completes all of their pages, they can share, comparing and contrasting.

Sample Applications

Science
- A certain type of rock or scientist

Social Studies
- Historical figure or a political party

Geography
- Country or city profile

World Language
- Country, author, historical figure, featured verb, fictional character

Math
- Formulas, theorems

English
- Character (fictional/nonfictional), author

Implementation Considerations

- By assigning concepts or individuals to students, you can differentiate for various student abilities and interests.
- To support study skills, you may select the most pertinent "Facebook" pages and create study packets and study questions based on them.
- Students can be paired or placed in small groups and work cooperatively for support or social experience.
- Some students can be assigned the same name or concept and then meet up to compare and contrast "Facebook" pages with students with the same assignment.

How This Strategy Can Support Individuals With Learning Differences

- This strategy supports the adolescent as it provides structured social learning experiences.
- This strategy provides a template to organize and showcase ideas and concepts for those with cognitive concerns.
- Students may be assigned different names or concepts based on ability.
- Visual and auditory presentations support different learning modalities.
- The products from this strategy can be used as study guides to support skills and memory.

Vignette Sample: English and Greek Mythology

In a seventh grade class, Mrs. S. introduced a unit on Greek mythology. After reading several myths and identifying characterization of many gods and goddesses, each student was assigned one mythological name. Female students were assigned goddesses, and males were assigned gods. Mrs. S. shared a "Facebook" page sample with the students to use as a model. "Facebook" pages included basic information, education, and work, likes and interests, and friends. An image of the god or goddess had to be included on the "Facebook" page.

When students completed "Facebook" pages, Mrs. S. made the class a Face Place. Students were eager to share "Facebook" pages, enthusiastically laughing and carrying on while sharing. Mrs. S. then told the class that, in 10 minutes, they'd have to pair and share with a partner, explaining why they would or would not "friend" that god or goddess. Students shared in pairs, referring to information on one another's "Facebook" pages.

Mrs. S. then selected exemplary "Facebook" pages with pertinent information and created a resource packet that students could refer to throughout the mythology unit and to use as a study guide at the end of the unit before the culminating examination.

"Only he can understand what a farm is, what a country is, who shall have sacrificed part of himself to his farm or country, fought to save it, struggled to make it beautiful. Only then will the love of farm or country fill his heart."
– Antoine de Saint-Exupery (1900–1944)

Information

Relationship
Status: Single

Currency City: Mount Olympus, Greece

Friends

11 Friends See all

Zeus

Poseidon

Hera

Persephone

Likes

Mount Olympus

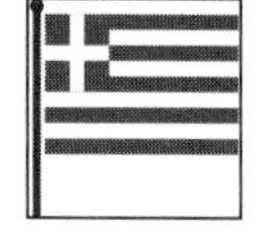

I <3 Greece

Demeter

Wall Info

About Me

Basic Info	Sex: Female Siblings: My sisters are Hestia and Hera. My brothers are Zeus and Hades.
Relationship	Not married; had an affair with Iason Status: Single Interested in: Men and crops Looking for: Persephone to come back from the Underworld Current City: Mount Olympus, Greece

Favorite Quotations

1) "All beautiful and noble qualities have been united in me . . . I shall be the fruit which will leave eternal vitality behind even after its decay. How great must be your joy, therefore, to have given birth to me."
—Egon Schiele

2) "I believe a leaf of grass is no less than the journey-work of the stars."
—Walt Whitman

Education and Work

Position: Goddess of harvest
Description: Decides when Greece's crops will be harvested; in charge of the grasses, grains, and fresh fruits

Likes and Interests

Activities: Watching grass grow, eating my favorite fruits, making a bountiful harvest, gardening, being with daughter Persephone

Interests: Gardening, healthy cooking, flying over steep rocky mountains, looking for good farmland

Music: Old McDonald Had a Farm by Irish Folk People; anything country; Strange Fruit by Billie Holiday; anything from the movie *Grease*

Books: *Country Life: A Handbook for Realists and Dreamers*; *Hobby Farming for Dummies* by Theresa A. Husarik; *History Alive Textbook: The Ancient World* by Teachers Curriculum Institute

Movies: *My Big Fat Greek Wedding*, *My Life in Ruins*, *The 300 Greek Spartans*, *Grease*

Television: *Healthy Appetite With Ellie Kreger*, any History Channel specials about Ancient Greece, *Greek*

STRATEGY 11

Framework

Explanation

This strategy is based on many years of teaching, which brought the realization that, during small group work, handing our students a piece of paper with the framework of the task already written on it appears to bring added focus to the task at hand. This is particularly useful in an inclusion classroom.

Materials

- Paper
- Computer and printer

Advance Preparation

- Make up handouts, a paper plan.

Directions

1. Prepare visual framework based on learning objectives. (See examples below.)
2. Get students into groups.
3. At the start of the process, hand out the papers you have prepared. Depending on the assignment, you can give out one per group or one per person.
4. The crux of this strategy is simply the paper you have prepared.
5. Inserting tables on your worksheet (using the insert tab on Word on your computer) is one effective way to organize answers and help students to realize the connections between each part of their answers.

Sample Applications

This strategy works for any subject matter in which you have the need to say, "Take out a paper and pencil, put your heading on it, and compose a list of . . . give three examples of . . ." and so on. This is especially effective for small group work.

Implementation Considerations

- It is not realistic to expect that, every single time you want students to work in groups or you need them to write down information, you are going to have a visual framework already prepared for them. There are times when you will need to say, "Take out a piece of paper. Put on your heading and . . ."

That said, there are lessons where it will be most valuable to have this strategy in place. Consider this for times like these:

- The ways students have been grouped, some of the personality combinations may result in more exuberance than required or desired.
- There is a fixed amount of time to complete the task.
- The assignment requires higher-order thinking and reflection, and you want to see the process the group goes through to get to the final answer (your framework can provide space so that they show all the steps along the way).
- You have students who have organizational issues or who take time to get started on the work or both.
- You want to keep groups accountable and on task, keeping the conversation on point and off of plans for the following weekend.

- You can ask a student to make up the visual framework for an upcoming lesson, allowing for some creative or artistic expression.

How This Strategy Can Support Individuals With Learning Differences

- This strategy supports students with organizational issues because the student is charged with filling in delineated spaces as opposed to looking at a blank page. The organizational structure is already completed.
- It helps students to utilize and reinforce metacognitive strategies.
- The most interesting part about this strategy in action is that it works for most students in most situations. When presented with a visual framework on paper, when all they have to do is read it, discuss, and fill in the answers, students seem to settle down and get to work more quickly. This supports students with attention issues and difficulty focusing for this reason.

Vignette Sample (All Grades, All Subjects)

Mr. X. was pleased, for the most part, with his tenth grade English class. As a group, they had lively conversations and came up with creative interpretations of what they read in class. They worked reasonably well on group projects, but there was room for improvement, specifically in the starting phase. He noticed that some of his students took a while to get started—dawdling, talking, getting themselves and the paper organized, choosing who was going to do what, and so on.

After the class read Huckleberry Finn, *he decided to get them into groups to discuss each character in the novel. Previously, he would have given directions, told them what to discuss, taken notes on their discussion, and explained that they would have 30 minutes and then all the groups would share. He decided, instead, to use a framework modeled after the examples on pages 87–89.*

Mr. X. passed out the framework to each group and observed. He noted that there were no major personality changes, the same individuals took charge, the louder group was still the louder group, and so on. He did realize, however, that each group settled down more quickly than usual, and they kept working. They had fewer questions for him and seemed to grasp the assignment well. And the bonus was that Mr. X. had this template on his computer, so the next time around, all he had to do was run it off.

After using the framework three or four times, the students became accustomed to using it and asked for one when it was not provided. He was particularly interested to note that, when he did not provide a framework, two groups actually created their own before they got down to the discussion of the topic.

EXAMPLE I

Names of group members: ____________, ____________, ____________, ____________

Date: ____

The novel we read was ________________. The date it was written is ________________.
The time period the novel is set in is ________________.

If this novel was set in the present day, the following changes would take place:

Example	How it was portrayed in the novel	How it would be portrayed today

Example 2

Name ____

Date ____

Topic: ____

List five facts:

1.
2.
3.
4.
5.

Which one fact were you most surprised about? Why? Please support your answer.

Relate one fact to something we learned about previously.

EXAMPLE 3

Names of group members: ____________, ____________, ____________, ____________

Date: ______________________________________

Topic: ______________________________________

Observations	Examples

STRATEGY 12

Information Rings

Explanation

Using index cards and key rings, students create their own information rings that provide review and reinforcement of academic content from any discipline, particularly that which has to be learned to automaticity.

Materials

- Index cards
- Hole punch
- Markers

or

- Information printed on paper (and glue)
- Key rings (buy from a dollar store, or send a note home at the beginning of the year and ask parents to send in any extra key rings they may have in the house)

Advance Preparation

- Identify the learning objectives related to key concepts for the content area, and decide on the information you want students to put on the cards.
- Students will be putting together their own information key rings.
- Decide how students will obtain the content for their information cards. You can disseminate the information, or the students can research the necessary information.

Directions

1. Distribute the materials for students to create their information cards.
2. Information may be written or cut and pasted from word processor documents.
3. It is important that the students create the cards themselves.
4. Instruct students to put a term on one side of the card with the corresponding information on the back of the same card (e.g., a vocabulary word goes on the front and the definition of that word goes on the back of the same card).
5. Students punch a hole in one corner of each card and attach the cards to a key ring. Yarn, twist ties, or pipe cleaners may be used as substitutes for key rings.
6. Cards may be laminated for durability and permanent use.
7. Individually, in pairs, or in groups, students can use the cards to study the terms.

Sample Applications

English

- Vocabulary words, characters, for example, from Shakespeare, where it may be difficult to remember names and roles
- Prefixes, suffixes, or roots—on one side put the prefix, for example, and on the other side write what the prefix means

Math

- Formulas, definitions of terms or symbols

Social Studies

- Historical events, people, campaign platforms, documents, and treaties

Science

- Vocabulary words

Implementation Considerations

Grouping

- This can be used with individuals or small groups.

Design

- Depending on the content used, you may want to put information on only one side of each card (e.g., spelling words or sight words).
- Laminating the cards is suggested when feasible.

Application

- Information Rings can both enhance and provide a model for effective study skills.
- This is an in-class strategy that can easily be transitioned for use in the home.

How This Strategy Can Support Individuals With Learning Differences

- You can prepare the information for the Information Rings to meet individual levels and learning needs as each student constructs his or her own key ring. There is no stigma attached because everyone has a key ring, and the differentiation (different words or content) is not obvious.
- Many skills need to be learned to automaticity, and information rings provide the opportunity for needed practice and review, which is particularly important for students with learning needs. Repetition helps content move from short-term to long-term memory for efficient retrieval. This supports memory.
- Information Rings support students with organizational skill deficits because, once constructed, the key ring is self-contained with no loose papers to lose or drop.

Vignette Sample: Verbal SAT Prep

In preparation for the SAT verbal examination, Mrs. V. gave students weekly vocabulary lists beginning in September of their junior year. She asked all students to bring in two 100 packs of index cards. She provided the hole punch and the key rings. Students were asked to define words on the index cards with the word on the front and the definition on the back. In addition, she asked that students use them in a number of ways, such as sentences, stories, and even plays. Each time new vocabulary was introduced, Mrs. V. asked students to add words to their Information Rings. Intermittently, students had time to review the cards for five to ten minutes in class, sometimes checking and quizzing each other. Mrs. V. gave intermittent vocabulary quizzes as well. When it came time for pre-SAT exams and the spring SAT exams, students had Information Rings available for study and review. Mrs. V. is well known for her SAT vocabulary development in the school, and students and teachers in senior year often continue to reference the rings as an effective study tool for continued SAT preparation.

STRATEGY 13

Invention Convention

Explanation

With the unit of study providing the context, students design inventions to meet a perceived need. Students identify a real-life problem and create an invention that addresses and solves the problem.

Materials

- Assorted craft materials, optional
- Cardboard boxes of a variety of sizes, including cardboard tubes, optional
- Poster board, masking tape, scissors, optional
- Recycled materials of all kinds—ask students to bring these in, optional

Directions

1. Decide on your topic. Discuss, as a class, the time period in question. Talk about the situation, possible problems that exist, or the issues that need to be resolved. Brainstorm. Write some ideas on the board.
2. Remind students that, when we face a problem, or something that could function better than it does currently, we look for a solution or another way to handle the situation. In this case, we are going to design an invention that will address the issue at hand. Encourage students to use their imaginations.
3. Get students into pairs or groups of three. Charge each group with identifying one problem or issue (related to the topic) that they want to tackle, and let them brainstorm ways to go about addressing that problem.
4. Each group needs to come up with an invention that will help the character in the novel, the historical figure, or the geographical area of the country, for example.
5. Give students ample time to think up concepts and then construct their inventions. Alternately, students can draw rough sketches and write out directions for construction.
6. Students have to explain, in writing or orally, why they came up with their inventions—what needs they address and how the inventions work.

Variation

- Students consider a period of history, or a novel from another century, or even just a decade earlier. Working individually or in groups, students rewrite the story in the context of modern times so that the characters in history or in literature have access to modern-day conveniences (i.e., technology). Rather than designing inventions to meet a perceived need, students explore how that perceived need could have been met with inventions that exist today. Illustrations can accompany the story.

Sample Applications

Social Studies/American History

- Consider the presidential election of 2000 where Bush and Gore were running and the votes were compromised because of difficulties at the election site, hanging chads, unspecified issues in Florida, and so on. The winner could not be immediately determined because of this situation. What invention could you design that would be able to eliminate this problem?

Science

- Geography/topography/weather—dream up an invention that prevents areas from flooding (consider tsunamis, for example).

Environmental Science

- Address issues surrounding the management of the Earth's water resources.

World Language

- Consider an invention that converts speech from the language someone is speaking into words in a language that the person listening can understand (that is, I say three sentences in English, speaking the words into my invention, and the words actually come out of the invention in fluent Japanese).

Health

- Focus on inventions to prevent disease (e.g., AIDS) or to support wellness (e.g., a machine that exercises for us but our bodies reap the benefits).

Service Learning

- As one component of a service learning project, which combines community service with academic objectives that relate to standards, have students design an invention that addresses the needs identified as part of the project.

Implementation Considerations

- The open-ended nature of this strategy lends itself to a multitude of ideas. Students can be as creative as they choose. The student who relishes a challenge can take this one and run with it.
- The timing of this strategy can vary widely. You can do it in one class period, with students discussing content, identifying the need they want to tackle, and then working in small groups to talk out an invention that would address or solve the problem. Alternately, this can take place over the time span of a week, with students actually creating their inventions, or

at least mock-ups, and coming up with written descriptions of what they are and how they work. You can devote some class time and some time at home for this to happen. This strategy can even have a longer time span, taking place over the course of a specific unit of study.

- This strategy can be paired with a particular unit of study, and the culminating lesson for the unit can be an Invention Convention where students share and explain their inventions.
- This strategy can be paired with the opportunity to write one or more of the various types of essays.
- To tie in an additional writing assignment, students can write letters to companies or investors convincing them of the reasons to fund and build this invention and put it on the market.

How This Strategy Can Support Individuals With Learning Differences

- The open-ended nature of this strategy invites creativity and out-of-the-box thinking and encourages higher-order thinking. This supports a variety of different types of learners who thrive in this type of situation. Students can be challenged.
- The Invention Convention Template provides the steps to help students to organize their thinking.
- The students who work better with their hands than their words benefit from this opportunity as well. They are able to pair a strength (developing an idea, designing or building something) with an area that needs some practice, explaining the problem and the solution they have come up with, orally or in writing.
- Impulsivity may be a plus when designing an invention, and that nature of the strategy is appealing to students who may have difficulties with attention.
- This strategy is designed for small groups. You may choose to have students work in pairs instead, or individually, or you can offer a choice.
- This strategy focuses on identifying a problem and brainstorming solutions. This is a way of thinking that benefits all students in middle school, in high school, in college, and in life.

Vignette Sample: Environmental Science and Pollution

Mrs. J.'s Environmental Science class was studying pollution. They started by examining several facts about pollution, and then as a class they generated a list, including water pollution, air pollution, car pollution, global warming, and litter.

Mrs. J. explained the Invention Convention strategy to the class and had them get into groups of three. She knew that Sam preferred to work by himself, so she spoke to him privately before the lesson started. She asked that he begin the process with one of the groups, which would give them a total of four people. Sam was asked to do the brainstorming with his group and come up with his own idea, and then he was given permission to construct his own invention based on one of the problems that the group came up with.

(Continued)

(Continued)

Each group was asked to decide which type of pollution or which pollution issue they wanted to tackle, and then they had to use the school library or classroom computers to do research on it. The next stage was for the group to generate a list of problems associated with this type of pollution. When this part was completed, each group decided which of the problems they generated that they wanted to tackle, and then they got down to work.

They were asked to design an invention that addressed and hopefully solved the problem at hand. Andrea's group was particularly concerned with all of the disposable materials being added to landfills yearly. As they researched further, they were astounded by the huge numbers of foam cups, tires, and diapers thrown away each year and started discussing how an invention could begin to address this problem.

Artie's group was interested in global warming and learned a lot from their research. They easily generated several problems but had to work long and hard to come up with any type of invention that might begin to address the issue.

The groups worked hard, and as Mrs. J. circulated, she heard some interesting discussions taking place. She urged them to take notes because this lesson would be continued at the next class period. At that time, the groups began to construct likenesses of their inventions from all of the materials Mrs. J. had assembled. The class was invited to bring in their own materials if they wanted as well, and several students did just that.

One group felt that their invention could best be represented by a picture, so they used a large poster board, sketched the invention with all of its requisite parts, and glued on pieces such as knobs, buttons, and wires as needed. They were pleased with their results.

For the final stage of this strategy, Mrs. J. asked each group to show their inventions and explain how they worked and how they addressed a particular pollution problem. She was impressed with the final products as well as with how knowledgeably each group spoke. The rest of the class asked thoughtful questions.

Mrs. J. reflected on the strategy. She felt that her students learned a lot and that they had a good understanding of the more complex issues surrounding pollution and the potential solutions. Her students were particularly motivated and worked well in groups. The one concern she had was the amount of time that the Invention Convention took. She realized that she had the time available for this unit, but for another unit, she would be able to modify the process using the strategy template, asking the students to write out how the invention would work and letting them draw the designs as opposed to constructing the entire invention. She was glad to realize she was able to modify this.

Invention Convention Template

Names of group members: ____________, ____________, ____________, ____________

Topic: ____

Name of Invention: ____

What did you learn from your research?

1.

2.

3.

List the problems you found that need to be addressed, and circle the one that you are going to base your invention on.

Explain how your invention works and how it addresses the problem that you identified. (This is in addition to the drawing or physical representation of your invention, which you will construct.)

STRATEGY 14

Jigsaw

Explanation

This is a cooperative learning experience where students begin in a home group and separate into other work groups to find information. Each student then returns to his or her home group to teach his or her peers what they've learned.

Advance Preparation

- Identify home group participants.
- Create different concept topics for students to participate in work groups.

Directions

1. Divide students into five- or six-person Jigsaw home groups.
2. Appoint one student from each group as the leader. Initially, this person should be the most mature student in the group.
3. Identify five to six concepts the students need to learn about.
4. Assign each student in the home group to learn about one specific concept. Number that concept.
5. Form temporary work groups by having one student from each Jigsaw home group join other students assigned to the same numbered concept.
6. Students move into work groups with those who have the same number and concept to explore. Students research, discuss, and record information in work groups.
7. When students are ready and you signal for transition, students from work groups return to their original home groups.
8. Each student presents his or her information to the group and encourages others in the group to ask questions for clarification.
9. At the end of the session, have students hand in completed data sheets with all group information for evaluation.

Sample Applications

All subjects with multiple concepts related to one topic

English
- Comparisons of authors, defining and exploring different genres

Math
- Specific review questions for an examination, for example, SAT review practice

Social Studies
- Information about a historical figure or event

Science
- Concepts related to different units of study such as global warming, natural disasters, types of energy, landforms, and so on

Implementation Considerations

- Assign concepts or topics to students with different functioning levels as appropriate.
- Pair students to go out to work groups, so no one needs to feel the pressure of misinforming home groups when they present new information learned.
- Provide students with graphic organizers to support concept development and presentation.

How This Strategy Can Support Individuals With Learning Differences

- This traditional cooperative learning strategy is ideal for adolescent learners as it allows students to learn in multiple social experiences with a purpose and the support of their peers.
- Jigsaw allows students to learn and repeat information for reinforcement and rehearsal.
- This strategy supports students with attention needs as they use movement and interaction in multiple groups.
- This strategy also supports community building among students as they rely on one another to learn information to complete assignments.

Vignette Sample: Social Studies and American History

Ms. H. was teaching a unit on famous women in history for Women's History Month. She chose Eleanor Roosevelt for the focus of the daily lesson. Ms. H. grouped six students in five mixed-ability Jigsaw groups. Students were given handouts with information they needed to learn about. She numbered each part of the handout as follows:

1. *Childhood*
2. *Her family life with Franklin and children*
3. *Her life after Franklin contracted polio*
4. *Her work in the White House as First Lady*
5. *Her life and work after Franklin's death*
6. *How Eleanor Roosevelt is memorialized and remembered today*

Each student was assigned a number to explore information related to a specific time in Eleanor Roosevelt's life. Ms. H. then directed students to break into their prospective work groups numbered one through six. In work groups, students could use texts, class computers, or any other reference material available to research specific concepts. After 20 minutes of researching and recording information, students were directed to return back to their original home groups. Individual students shared information learned in their work

(Continued)

(Continued)

groups. Students in home groups completed data sheets and turned them in to Ms. H. for assessment.

The following day, Ms. H. distributed graded group data sheets about Eleanor Roosevelt and allowed groups an opportunity to share information with the class in a review.

Resource

Aronson, E. (2000–2012). Jigsaw in 10 easy steps. *Jigsaw Classroom* (website). Social Psychology Network. Retrieved from http://www.jigsaw.org/steps.htm

STRATEGY 15

Linked-In

Explanation

This strategy provides an opportunity for students to share and defend like opinions as they collaboratively share supporting information.

Materials

- Large poster paper
- Tape
- Markers

Directions

1. Ask the class to make a decision. They can agree, disagree, infer, analyze, or evaluate a situation or problem.
2. Students write their responses to your query with details to support their points of view.
3. Students then walk around the class and share their perspectives with peers, seeking individuals with like perspectives.
4. Once groups of students with similar points of view "link" in groups, give each a large poster paper and marker.
5. Together, students in groups write their viewpoints as headings on the top of their poster papers and list all the supporting information below.
6. Students share opinions to support viewpoints with the class.

Sample Applications

English

- Inferences about a character, action, conclusion, or prediction from literature; information to support persuasive expository writing

Science

- Describing the purpose or solution to chemistry or physics problems, creating hypotheses for science experimentation

Social Studies

- Taking positions on social issues and possible solutions, such as terrorism and failing economies

Math

- Comparing multiple ways to solve a problem

Implementation Considerations

- Other forms of documentation or visuals, instead of posters, may be used; for example, groups can make webpages or create political cartoons or pictures to convey their points of view. If there are too many students with the same view, create multiple groups with the same perspectives. It will be interesting to learn if they have varied rationales.

How This Strategy Can Support Individuals With Learning Differences

- As needed, preteach or reteach (to the whole class or selected individuals) how to infer, analyze, or evaluate a situation or problem.
- This strategy provides a social learning experience with movement and cooperative learning to support attention deficits and encourage appropriate social interaction.
- Allowing students with metacognitive issues to share ideas creates an opportunity to debate and develop information and inferences with supporting details.

Vignette Sample: English—*Of Mice and Men*

After reading the novel Of Mice and Men *by John Steinbeck, Mrs. E. asked her students to decide what the theme of the book was and why. She allowed students to use their notes and books to determine the theme. Once the students were done writing their responses, she asked them to walk around the class and "link" in with the other students who shared their opinions.*

Students walked around and linked in with individuals with similar responses. Once students found their groups, Mrs. E. provided three different groups with pieces of large poster paper and black markers. Students discussed their viewpoints and placed their answers on the large paper, listing supporting information.

The three themes that were developed and shared included the following:

Man Is Competitive and Out for Himself

- *Curley's wife flirts and gets men in trouble because she is bored and wants attention.*
- *Curley picks on Lennie because he wants to feel powerful.*
- *Ranch men put down Crooks because he is black and they want to believe they are better than him.*
- *George kills Lennie because he doesn't want any more trouble around him.*
- *Carlson takes advantage of Candy by convincing him to let Carlson kill his dog.*

Friendship Is Powerful

- *George and Lennie are better than all the other ranchers because they have each other.*
- *George and Lennie have survived all these years because they looked out for each other. Lennie would have never been hired and made money if it weren't for George helping him.*
- *Other ranchers are jealous that George and Lennie have each other and wish they weren't homeless and lonely.*

- *George kills Lennie out of love for a friend, so he doesn't have to be imprisoned or killed for killing Curley's wife.*

The American Dream Is Impossible

- *Lennie and George can never get the ranch they dream of no matter how hard they work.*
- *Candy has the dream of owning a ranch and doesn't fulfill it.*
- *Curley's wife has the dream of getting married and living happily ever after, and she is lonely and unloved.*
- *Crooks has a dream of owning land one day, and he has no respect because he is black and he is not successful.*

Mrs. E. found students engaged and enthusiastic to participate. When students ran out of ideas, she assisted by allowing them to use the book and notes as a reference and by asking probing questions. When students were done, they designated a reporter to share their responses. Poster papers were hung on the walls as a visual support. One of the essay questions on Mrs. E.'s exam was to explain one theme in Of Mice and Men. *This activity supported student knowledge of the big ideas from this course of study.*

STRATEGY 16

Listening Teams

Explanation

Throughout this book, we have explored interactive strategies designed to engage students in their own learning. We freely acknowledge that different types of lessons lend themselves best to different strategies. Listening Teams (Silberman, 1996) is most effective for those times when you need to use direct teaching, like a lecture approach, to get a certain body of material across. At the same time, the need for student involvement is still a priority. This is particularly applicable in the middle and high school setting where lecture is a typical part of the instructional repertoire.

For this strategy, each group is given one question or issue to report on when you are finished speaking.

According to Mel Silberman (1996), "Listening teams create small groups responsible for clarifying the class material."

Materials

- Index cards, one per group
- Pens, pencils, markers

Advance Preparation

- Decide how you will group the students in the class. Each group will focus on a different question or topic.
- Choose from the following focus questions, and write each question on a separate index card, one for each small group:
  - List three facts that you just learned.
  - Write down three questions that you have.
  - Explain how you would apply the information you just heard, or give examples to show your understanding.
  - List a few things that the teacher covered that your group did not know before this lesson.
  - Take something that the teacher talked about, and explain it in a different way.
  - Relate what the teacher talked about to something from a previous lesson on the same topic.
  - Write down something you disagree with, and explain why. If there is nothing you disagree with, then explain why not.
  - Is there a theme or message to this lesson?
  - What would you like to know more about? What resources would you use to find out?
  - How can you connect something you learned in this lesson to another subject area?

Directions

1. Assemble students into small groups, and give each group an index card with a focus question on it before you begin the lesson. Explain that this is what they will need to address after you have finished the lecture.
2. Teach the lesson.
3. Give groups a few minutes to collaborate and write out their answers.
4. Let each group take a turn explaining what they have written, and give the class an opportunity to respond to what each group says. This serves as an in-depth review of the lecture. You can clarify information as needed.

Sample Applications

American Literature
- The use of symbolism in the 20th-century novel

Social Studies/American History
- Taxes and tariffs
- The three branches of government
- The causes and effects of the Cold War

Science
- Bacteriological warfare
- The scientific method
- The genesis of natural disasters
- Zoology—animals without backbones

Health
- Symptoms, possible causes, and available treatments for mental health disorders

Economics
- The barter economy and how it works

World Language
- The questions on the index cards can be written in the students' native language or in the language being studied

Implementation Considerations

Grouping
- You may want to use four questions but eight groups, so each question is addressed twice.

Timing
- The timing of the direct instruction portion of the lesson corresponds to the topic at hand as well as the age, attention span, and ability level of the class. For example, for a science lesson, you may want to spend the first

15 to 20 minutes building the foundation of information through direct instruction, use this strategy to reinforce the content, and then finish with an experiment that demonstrates the process.

How This Strategy Can Support Individuals With Learning Differences

- Providing a focus for students as they listen to the teacher talking encourages both attention and accountability. It affords another way for students to stay engaged during a lesson.
- Listening Teams supports individuals with auditory processing issues because students hear the concept orally multiple times, first as the teacher is teaching it and then again as groups take turns explaining the answers to each index card. As students share what they have written down, the key concepts are repeated once more, this time in oral bullet points, reinforcing what they needed to be listening for.
- This strategy helps to clarify questions students might have as they listen to the lecture.
- Listening Teams provides a framework for questions and answers and for students to engage with the content as they listen, while at the same time, it allows the teacher to go through a chunk of material. This supports students who may call out questions impulsively or continuously.

Vignette Sample: American Literature

Mrs. P. was beginning a unit on the American novel throughout different periods of history in terms of both social themes and writing style. She planned to emphasize the literature of each time period within its historical context. In preparation for the lesson, she typed each question on an index card and distributed one card per group of four.

She felt that a lecture was the best way to get across a large amount of content knowledge, but she was concerned that the students wouldn't be able to stay attentive and absorb and apply the information that they heard. As part of her lecture, she explained several clues that students could use when looking at literature to relate what they read to the time in which the novel was set. She developed a set of questions to help students focus on these ideas as they listened and to provide reinforcement of these key ideas as each group shared their answers following the lecture.

She was pleased with student responses at the end of her lecture, when each group discussed the questions on their index cards. She found that students listened well, shared insights into the subject matter, and brought up some points she had not thought of. A few times, she was able to clarify information. After Mrs. P. used this strategy a few times and students were comfortable with it, she asked students if they were able to focus better with an index card question and, if so, why.

Resource

Silberman, M. (1996). *Active learning: 101 strategies to teach any subject.* Needham Heights, MA: Allyn & Bacon.

STRATEGY 17

Next

Explanation

In this strategy, students work together to reconstruct a reading or other assignment. Students take turns sharing their understanding or knowledge of a particular topic in a fast-paced experience to create an order of events.

Materials

- Text
- Homework assignments, notebooks, or other subject area resources

Advance Preparation

- Students must complete an assignment.

Directions

1. Have students complete an assignment independently in class or at home.
2. Select specific information you want students to share and review with one another.
3. Instruct a student, with assignment in hand, to begin talking about the topic from the beginning, such as the beginning of a story or the beginning of an approach to a math problem.
4. Signal the next student to continue where the previous student left off.
5. The next student continues to explain or share from where the previous student left off. Each student only shares one or two sentences related to the topic.
6. The next student picks up where the previous student left off.
7. The chain continues until the entire assignment or specific problem is covered.
8. Typically this strategy uses a chain of four to six students.

Sample Applications

Math
- ○ Solving parts of an equation together or solving a word problem

Science (Chemistry or Physics)
- ○ Setting up a problem using a specific formula and solving it

Social Studies
- Reviewing the sequence of historical or current events

English
- Walking through a plot of a story, chapter, or novel

World Language
- Translating a text

Implementation Considerations

- Select student order considering student ability. For example, if the beginning or end of a story or problem is easier to share, allow students with less confidence or ability to participate in that part of the chain.
- If students have trouble with speed or content, you can preteach specific topic information to prepare students to be successful in participation.
- Students can use any resource, such as their notes or the text, to help them construct an order of events.
- Students can pass or "phone a friend" if they have difficulty responding. Remember, because this is a fast-paced assignment, there is little time for a person called upon to procrastinate.
- This assignment can be used as a formative assessment opportunity to determine which students are completing reading or homework assignments and have mastered learning objectives.

How This Strategy Can Support Individuals With Learning Differences

- Students who did not understand the reading or problem assigned can benefit from the Next student.
- Students who have memory issues have an opportunity to hear or repeat information themselves for rehearsal and reinforcement.
- This brief, fast-paced strategy keeps students engaged and interested as they need to listen and take turns to be a successful participant.
- The auditory learning experience benefits students with visual processing concerns.

Vignette Sample: World Social Studies—China

Mr. M. assigned his Social Studies class a reading on the May Fourth Movement in China. When the students returned to class the following day, he told the class that they could take out the reading from the evening before as the class was going to participate in the Next strategy for review. Sally was asked to be the first student to start off. Sally mentioned that "the Taiping Rebellion led to the May Fourth Movement." Mr. M. motioned to Billy, sitting behind Sally, to pick it up from there. Billy spoke about the building of railroads in China, thus showing government reform. After Billy finished his sentence, Mr. M. pointed to Samantha. Samantha stumbled, searching the text for an appropriate contribution. Because it was a fast-paced strategy, Mr. M. asked her if she'd like to pass or "phone a friend." She quickly motioned to her neighbor Steven, and he answered for her in correct chronological order. Next continued as four more students mentioned various events that led to the May 4, 1919, Chinese student protests.

This strategy provided an opportunity for students to review material and provided Mr. M. with the knowledge that the students comprehended the homework reading passage and could identify the main concepts related to this historical event.

STRATEGY 18

Philosophical Chairs

Explanation

Students present different sides of a debate, sitting on opposite sides of the room, trying to persuade others to change their opinions and move to their side.

Materials

- Note-taking sheets

Advance Preparation

- Select a critical thinking question related to the topic of study.
- Ask students to create notes that reflect their perspectives.
- Set up chairs on either side of the room with some in the middle for those students who remain undecided.

Directions

1. Ask students to respond to a critical thinking question that asks them each to choose one side of an argument.
2. Students prepare notes and supporting statements related to a stance in the debate.
3. Ask students to take seats on either side of the classroom, indicating which side of the debate they have selected to support.
4. Hot seats are placed in the middle of the classroom for those students who are undecided.
5. A mediator selects students to speak, making sure that three different students speak before the same student is allowed to share again.
6. After each student speaks, the mediator allows time for each student to choose a side or change his or her mind.
7. When everyone has had time to respond, students are asked to write a reflection related to their participation and learning experience in the philosophical chair debate.

Philosophical Chairs Classroom Design

Side A	Hot Seats	Side B
X		X
X	X	X
X		X

X	X	X
X		X
X	X	X
X		X
X		X

Sample Applications

Science/Health

- Do you believe the drinking age should be lowered to 18?
- Do you believe most people care enough about the environment to make personal sacrifices to save it?

Social Studies

- Would you have hidden a Jewish family with your family during the Holocaust?
- Who would you vote for in a presidential election?

English

- Write a persuasive essay and defend your position; for example, "On the topic of abortion, are you pro-life or pro-choice?" or "Do you believe high schools should have child care services for students?"
- Given a specific character from a story or novel, ask students if they agree or disagree with the character's actions, or ask students if they believe the character acted appropriately or not, providing substantial details to support their responses.

Implementation Considerations

- A student or the teacher may moderate Philosophical Chairs.
- The number of hot seats may change depending on student response.
- You may decide not to use hot seats at all.
- You may assign students to present on different sides of the debate typically to even out the sides.
- Graphic organizers or note templates like Cornell Notes may be used to help students organize thoughts and present material.
- Provide students with directions for participation:
    - Active listening—Listen to others carefully even if you don't agree with their statement.
    - Summarize briefly the previous student's argument before making your own.
    - When you speak, address ideas and not the person who shared them.
    - Keep an open mind, and do not be embarrassed to move to the other side of the room.
    - Remain quiet until someone is finished speaking, and raise your hand and wait until the mediator calls on you before answering.

How This Strategy Can Support Individuals With Learning Differences

- This strategy supports the adolescent as it provides a structured social learning experience.
- Students may use notes and graphic organizers to ensure success when presenting information related to each side of the debate.
- Discussion supports individuals with visual learning issues.
- This strategy supports individuals with memory and study skill needs as it allows multiple opportunities to reinforce through note-taking, discussion and debate, and reflection.

Vignette Sample: English

While reading George Orwell's Animal Farm, *Mrs. C. asked the class to respond to the following. Which slogan will you support: "Vote for Snowball, the three day week and the use of pigeons" or "Vote for Napoleon, the full manger, and the use of firearms."*

She split the class into halves, dividing up students to support each slogan. Mrs. C. acted as the mediator, and hot seats were not used because everyone had a statement to support. Students used Cornell Notes outlines to prepare their arguments, and they were allowed to refer to these notes during Philosophical Chairs.

After Mrs. C. reviewed the student rules for participation, she began the debate by flipping a coin to determine which team would go first, and then asking for volunteers to share. Victoria spoke first from Snowball's side: "With Snowball's idea, the animals would have more time for leisure and to relax. They have already been overworked." Maddie from Napoleon's side shot back: "Yes, but animals would be poorly trained if they were only working three days a week! It would leave more time for the humans to come in and take over while everyone was off guard." Kayla, from the Snowball defense, was next to speak. "The worst part of Napoleon's idea is the use of firearms. Now, the animals are training to become killers instead of working on the farm. If they spend that amount of time training with firearms, how will the manger be filled with food?" Matt from Napoleon's side said, "But there is no way the animals can truly be protected with pigeons! Pigeons just stir up rebellions. It doesn't mean they can defend the animals." Lauren from Snowball's side returned, "Napoleon, who is cruel and mean, would make the animals overworked with no time off and use guns!" At that time, Tori and Ashley moved from Napoleon's side to Snowball's side. The students on Snowball's side began to cheer and clap for their victory. Mrs. C. calmed the class down and continued to provide an opportunity for everyone to speak, encouraging those more reticent to use their Cornell Notes for referral.

When everyone had spoken at least once, Mrs. C. summed the main arguments from each side for closure, asking everyone to write a reflection that evening for homework. The students were asked to write about what they learned during Philosophical Chairs and to explain why they would choose to remain on the side of the debate they were on or what they would do differently if they had to repeat this assignment. All reflections indicated that everyone, even the quietest students, enjoyed the engagement of Philosophical Chairs and could write about both sides of the debate adequately.

Resource

Duez, D. (2009). *Using philosophical chairs.* Retrieved from http://www.scribd.com/mrduez/d/12410807-Using-Philosophical-Chairs

STRATEGY 19

Photo Finish

Explanation

In a deductive reasoning strategy, students identify the steps that lead to a solution or a specific event. Students develop a sequence of events with index cards. The final index card is a picture representation of a conclusion.

Materials

- Envelopes
- Index cards for each group
- Illustrations or pictures as needed

Advance Preparation

- Prepare envelopes with index cards and pictures for specific groups.

Directions

1. Identify a cause-and-effect concept related to lesson objectives.
2. Place a visual, such as a picture, quote, cartoon, and so on, on one index card for each group.
3. Place five index cards in an envelope: four blank ones and one with the visual.
4. Divide the class in groups, and give each group an envelope.
5. Explain to the class they will receive five cards; only one has something on it. Using the four blank cards, determine how the information on the last card came about. Write down steps or circumstances in sequential order to arrive at the last card.
6. After distributing envelopes to groups, walk around, listening, directing, and facilitating when necessary.

Sample Applications

English
- ○ The final scene from a play or story, a quote from a character

Math
- ○ The solution to a problem, such as X = 7

Social Studies
- ○ Pictures of different events and experiences, famous quotes from historical figures

Science
- Pictures of fossils, the final part of the food chain, habitats, and so on

Implementation Considerations

- Prepare different level card information for different groups depending on functioning levels and interests.
- Use fewer or more cards requiring more or less detail based on functioning levels and concepts.
- Allow students to use resources as references to develop information.

How This Strategy Can Support Individuals With Learning Differences

- Starting at the end of a sequence of events and working backwards to construct how it came to be is a novel way to approach a task. This strategy provides an opportunity for discussion of cause and effect and gives groups the opportunity to work together toward a common goal.
- Visual pictures support students with auditory processing concerns.
- Review and reinforcement of a concept in sequential order provide support for those with memory issues.

Vignette Sample: American Revolution

In a review of the Revolutionary War unit, Mr. C. used the Photo Finish strategy. He asked students to work collaboratively to sequence facts that led to specific significant events. The class was placed in five groups, and each was given an envelope with a specific picture and four index cards labeled one to four. On each card, groups were asked to write down events that led to the final significant event—whatever was displayed in the photo. Students used their texts and notes to support their choices. Some examples of completed group cards are below.

When Mr. C. called time, students looked at the group next to them to see if their displays were correct, often having to check back in their notes. Mr. C. went around checking students and encouraging them to write more information and change card order if sequencing was not correct.

Mr. C. felt some groups worked significantly harder at finding information with supporting detail, and it was apparent that those groups benefitted the most from the strategy. He realized that he needed to provide more direction and a point assessment the next time he used the strategy.

GROUP A

1. Quartering Act

2. Stamp Act

3. Townsend Act

4. TEA Act

Boston Tea Party

Group B

1. 1754–1763: French and Indian War

   This war between Britain and France ended with the victorious British deeply in debt and demanding more revenue from the colonies. With the defeat of the French, the colonies became less dependent on Britain for protection.

2. 1763: Proclamation of 1763

   This prohibited settlement beyond the Appalachian Mountains. While Britain did not intend to harm the colonists, many colonists took offense at this order.

3. 1770: Boston Massacre

   The colonists and British soldiers openly clashed in Boston. This event was used as an example of British cruelty despite questions about how it actually occurred.

4. Continental Congress

   Representatives from 13 colonies met to discuss unfair treatment and high taxes from England.

Revolutionary War

STRATEGY 20

Playlist

Explanation

This strategy capitalizes on the adolescent's interest in music. Students work in groups to create a playlist that reflects the key themes of the content to be covered and then present their work to the class as a whole. Discussion of content ensues.

Materials

- Poster board
- Thin-tipped colored markers
- Other materials as needed, depending on what visual representation options your class has (and whether this part will be completed in class or at home)

Advance Preparation

1. You can make a sample visual representation if you choose to, using a topic other than the ones your students will use.
2. Make copies of the template below.

Directions

1. Introduce this strategy with a discussion of the ways in which music conveys messages. You may also want to discuss the differences in music from one era to the next.
2. Assign students to work in groups. Each group will develop a playlist that reflects the lesson content as the subject matter of each song.
3. Give each group a strategy template to work with.
4. Each group will be charged with the following:
    - Agreeing on a unifying name (title) for the playlist that is reflective of the content on which it is based
    - Designing a visual representation that reflects their playlist (i.e., video clip, collage, poster, CD cover)
    - Making up 10 song titles; the song titles all need to be related to the topic in some way
    - Writing out the full lyrics to one of the song titles and choosing the tune that will go with it (suggest they go with a common tune that everyone is familiar with)

5. Students generally need at least a good part of one class period to work on this strategy, and any additional work can be completed on their own time.

6. When the playlists are completed, take one class period for each group to present their work, which will include the singing of the song they wrote. (You can eliminate the actual singing requirement if you so choose.) Encourage discussion after each presentation. Focus on the themes and how they represent the lesson content.

7. As lesson closure, ask the class what they have learned about the topic, if any ideas were introduced that they had not previously considered, and what their current thoughts are.

Sample Applications

English
- Themes from the book that the class has just read:
  - *Tess of the D'Urbervilles*
  - *House on Mango Street*
  - *The Giver*

Social Studies
- The Great Depression
- Paul Revere
- Vietnam War and self-determination
- The parts of the Magna Carta
- Eleanor Roosevelt

Science
- Animals that are becoming extinct

Math
- Themes and terminology studied during the course as review

Implementation Considerations

- Begin this strategy by playing music that conveys a message, and ask students to describe what their reactions are to what they hear. (One possibility is to play protest songs and talk about their place in history.)
- If time is a concern, use just one part of this strategy (i.e., design a visual or develop a playlist or compose one song); you might choose to use this strategy a few times during the semester, using a different part of it each time.

How This Strategy Can Support Individuals With Learning Differences

- This strategy plays to a variety of different skills so that there is a greater possibility that each student's strengths will be a valuable piece of what needs to be done. It provides the opportunity for many different students to shine and to look competent in front of their peers as well as to develop self-confidence from a job well done.

- Music is commonly a strong interest of adolescents. This strategy is motivating and, as such, is a good choice for reluctant learners and those who might struggle in your particular subject.
- Because music is commonly a strong interest of adolescents, it may serve as a common denominator among your students. The topic has the potential to be inclusive, to bring in many different voices to the discussion, letting each voice be heard. Simply put, music can be a common ground that encourages conversation and encourages all students to be included as opposed to excluded from the group.
- This strategy encourages students to view content from a variety of perspectives, from lively small group discussions to choosing a unifying theme and song titles that are most reflective of content, to listening to the views of classmates throughout the group presentations. This strategy involves the art of compromise and listening skills as well as the opportunity to look at a topic from multiple perspectives.
- Use of the template helps students to organize their thinking.

Vignette Sample: English Literature

Ms. C. had her students create playlists based on the works of William Shakespeare. Each group approached the strategy from a different point of view. Each group discussed the subject in depth, deciding how to best use the material at hand and brainstorming what they knew about Shakespeare—the time period in which he wrote, the perception at the time of the role of women in society, whom he "borrowed" from, play construction, and the playwright's craft—in addition to discussing both the merits and basic elements of several of his plays.

Each group took a different approach, resulting in several unique presentations and an interesting class session in which each group performed their original songs and shared their work with classmates.

Upon reflection, Ms. C. felt that this strategy created a meaningful learning experience for her students because it allowed individuals to analyze and interpret concepts and share their own perceptions with peers. And she particularly enjoyed seeing the creativity (and senses of humor) in the final presentations.

Source: This strategy is inspired by a project designed by Beverly Carboy, a retired New Jersey high school English teacher.

The Playlist Template

Names of group members: ____________, ____________, ____________, ____________

The topic we are studying: ____

1. Consider the topic at hand. List the key themes that emerge.

2. Review your list above. Choose one of the themes, and list several things you know about this theme, including the facts, what it relates to, and real-world examples.

3. Based on 2, make up a song title that relates. Continue the process until you have 10 song titles.

4. Title your playlist.

5. Design a visual representation that reflects your playlist (i.e., video clip, collage, poster, CD cover). Make sure you keep your theme(s) in mind.

STRATEGY 21

Puzzle Pieces

Explanation

Pieces of related information are placed on different cards, and the cards are distributed to different students. To solve the puzzle, students walk around and talk to each other until they find matches for their cards. Classmates have the opportunity to agree, disagree, and debate matching puzzle choices.

Materials

- Cardstock or index cards
- Scissors
- Glue
- Envelopes (for cooperative activity groups)

Advance Preparation

- Identify the learning objectives related to the key concepts of the content area.
- Decide whether to give students the information on their index cards or ask students to research the information and hand it in to you.
- Print the information on one side of each card. Information can be printed on cardstock that is then cut into smaller cards or printed on paper and glued to index cards.
- Shuffle the cards before distribution, or place them in envelopes for cooperative groups.

Directions

1. Walk around the room handing a card or cards to random students.
2. Give students directions on how to organize the cards, depending on the lesson objectives. For example, they may need to match terms with definitions, sequence story events, or compile true-and-false statements.
3. Students either work in groups or work with the entire class.
4. Once students have determined which cards match or belong together, they let you know they are ready for evaluation.
5. You may ask classmates to discuss, debate, and defend card choices, or you may evaluate the card-matching choices.

Variation: Cooperative Groups

1. Two or more teams may be given the same set of mixed cards with information.

2. Place cards in envelopes, and provide one envelope to each cooperative learning group.
3. Each group has to arrange mixed Puzzles Pieces in an order that makes sense (e.g., terms and definitions, sequencing).
4. Other students and groups may be called on to examine and compare results with their own. Thus, a dialogue ensues to further the student-centered learning experience.
5. When teams are ready, in a class discussion, students review one another's work, comparing and contrasting matching decisions.

Sample Applications

English
- Vocabulary words and definitions, characters from literature, and characteristics or quotes

Math
- Mathematics symbols and their definition for use; math equations and their solutions, for example, $(5 + 4) \times 2$ written on one card and 18 on the corresponding card

Social Studies
- Causes and effects of wars or information about other historical events

Science
- Vocabulary and definitions, chemical or physics formulas, and problems and corresponding answers, any questions and answers related to material

World Language
- Any vocabulary and English translation, questions and answers in world language

Study Skills
- Student-created questions and answers for test questions, submitted to the teacher

Implementation Considerations

Design for Research/Inquiry Assignments
- Students may research new information to share with the class and submit information for cards to the teacher (e.g., students are assigned different branches of government and must write about their functions).
- In inquiry assignments, students design their own research questions related to a topic and submit responses for card matching and sharing.

Mixed Abilities
- Information on cards can be specifically distributed based on student ability to challenge and support where necessary.
- Cooperative groups can be formed purposefully.

How This Strategy Can Support Individuals With Learning Differences

- Cards provide visual support for students with auditory processing needs and language needs.
- Repetition and discussion supports memory.
- Students with social skill needs are provided a structure and purpose to interact appropriately.

Vignette Sample: Life Science—Bacteria

Mrs. S. was working on a unit about bacteria. She decided to use Puzzle Pieces to support instruction because this unit had many new terms. She typed up questions and answers and cut and pasted them onto index cards. She mixed up the cards and distributed them to the class, one card each. One student got two cards as a classmate was absent. There were 14 question cards and 14 answer cards, 28 total. Then, she told students to walk around and find their puzzle piece matches. If a student made a match, he or she had to post it to the bulletin board in front of the class. When students were done, they could sit down or help a friend in need, supporting other students who might be struggling to find their matches.

When the class successfully matched all cards, Mrs. S. directed student attention to the bulletin board. She read matching puzzle piece cards, and students could agree or disagree with the information. Questions such as "Define flagella, fission, *and* eubacteria*" were matched correctly with their definitions. Mismatched cards were* aerobe *and* anaerobe*. Students argued about the matches, and Mrs. S. let them use their texts to determine the correct matches. Students learned that an aerobe is a bacterium that requires oxygen and an anaerobe is a bacterium that lives without oxygen. To remember this concept, Juan, one of the students, said, "Remember the n in the word* anaerobe *means no oxygen."*

Mrs. S. used the same cards two more times for review and practice throughout the unit. It was not redundant for students. Each time, students were given different cards than they previously had. They found it exciting to quickly find matches as they had more confidence in their knowledge of terms. Mrs. S. found the Puzzle Pieces strategy supported diverse learners while making a once-daunting unit of study appealing!

STRATEGY 22

Reading Discussion Cards

Explanation

Playing cards represent discussion points for students working in small groups. This strategy provides the opportunity for students to discuss what they read informally but with an existing structure.

Materials

- A deck of cards, separated

Advance Preparation

- Prepare the list of discussion topics available, and next to each topic, put a corresponding number or picture name from a deck of cards.
- The discussion topic list can include the following:
  - What did you learn from the reading? Queen
  - What is your opinion of what you read? King
  - Explain one way in which you can relate what you read to your personal experience or to something you have learned before. Jack
  - Just chat, wherever the conversation takes you, as long as it stays on topic. Ace
  - If you had to explain what you read to a friend, what would you say? Ten
  - Based on what you have read, what else would you like to know? Nine
  - What questions do you have about what you read? Eight
- Sort out the deck of cards—if you are using six topics, as an example, then you will be using all of the nines, tens, jacks, kings, queens, and aces in the deck.

Directions

1. Get students into groups of three or four. Remind groups that they will be reflecting on the reading that they had for homework or something they have just read in class prior to getting into groups.

2. Let one person in each group choose a card—the type of card picked corresponds to the topic that the group will discuss. Give each group the list of topics so that they can find what they have been assigned to discuss.

3. Groups have 10 minutes to discuss what they have read. The discussion should center on the assigned topic.

4. There are three rules the groups need to follow:
   - Stay on topic.
   - Everyone has a chance to speak.
   - Practice nonjudgmental listening—all opinions count.

5. After 10 minutes, stop the conversation, and ask the group to take a minute to summarize the key points of the discussion.
6. Reconvene the class as a whole group, and let one or more people from each group share.
7. This thorough discussion of the reading can lead seamlessly into the next part of your lesson.

Variations

- Have all groups focus on the same discussion topic, or let the each group choose from the list of topics you have prepared.
- Assign roles within the group:
  - the leader (who starts the discussion and keep the group on task)
  - the scribe (who takes notes during the discussion)
  - the definition guru (who uses the dictionary on the computer or another resource to check definitions of words the group is unfamiliar with)
  - the summarizer (who summarizes the discussion into three or four main points)
  - the speaker (who shares with the class)
- Have two or more groups with the same discussion topic card, so they can compare, contrast, and add to each other's information during whole group discussion.

Sample Applications

Reading material in any subject area, including the class text, supplementary reading, articles, or a specific website, for example, reading a chapter about the five major religions in the world in a class on world cultures

Implementation Considerations

- Choose groups that have the potential to work well together, or allow students to choose their own groups once in a while.
- In your list of questions, consider including one totally unexpected topic that relates to the reading and that students may have a good time talking about.
- This is an effective way for students to review prior reading and set the stage for what is to be learned next.
- If a group finishes early, have them select another card from the pile and begin on a new discussion topic.
- Depending on the needs of your class, you can have students create lists of specific elements of nonjudgmental listening the first time you use this strategy, and then you can refer back to the list if needed throughout the semester.

How This Strategy Can Support Individuals With Learning Differences

- The informal flow of ideas among peers benefits all learners, and more reticent speakers may be encouraged to share thoughts in this setting more readily than in a whole group discussion. To capitalize on this, you may want to establish reading discussion groups that stay together for a month or more at a time.

- Provide students with graphic organizers to use to take notes with when each group shares (see example below). This helps students to organize the information that comes from the whole group discussion and creates a visual reference. You can give students a few minutes after everyone has shared to review and finish up the graphic organizers individually or as a group. The completed graphic organizers can double as study guides for an upcoming test.
- This strategy incorporates the socialization needs of adolescent learners with the need to manipulate and work with new material to make it their own.

Vignette Sample: Social Studies and American History

Mr. Q. assigned a reading for homework that discussed how the U.S. Constitution helped to protect the rights of the people by both empowering and limiting the federal government. Mr. Q. wanted his students to be familiar with the topic so that they could connect with the lesson and engage in discussion. Because the reading had a lot of content, Mr. Q. decided to use the Reading Discussion Card strategy at the beginning of the lesson to help students organize their thoughts based on their reading and to activate prior knowledge, again from their reading the previous evening.

He used the questions listed in the directions above but added two additional questions that related to his topic.

- *How is it possible to both empower and limit something, or someone, at the same time? Can this happen, or are they mutually exclusive of one another? Eight*
- *If you were on the committee, what would you have changed about the Constitution? Seven*

He also added one final question:

- *Choose any of the questions on the list to answer, or make up and answer your own question as it pertains directly to the reading. Six*

Mr. Q. distributed the lists and one playing card per group and let the groups get started. Students were animated, and a few times, he had to remind the groups to lower the noise level, but he was delighted to see the level of animation in his classroom. Students were avidly discussing their questions, sometimes disagreeing, often coming to consensus. During the group share, Mr. Q. was particularly pleased with the level of student involvement and the quality of the points that each group made. There were a few questions raised by peers, which sometimes group members were able to answer, and at other times, Mr. Q. was able to clarify the response. Students were intrigued with the idea of empowering and limiting power and how that worked and came up with many examples of how that relates to the current day, to political parties, to the school system, and to their own lives as well.

All in all, Mr. Q. was satisfied with the strategy. He asked the groups to share in sequential order, the order he would have used to cover the material himself. As each group shared, he was able to clarify, expand, and pose thoughtful questions on each point. This allowed him, essentially, to teach the lesson with maximum student participation and to continue on to introduce new content secure in the knowledge that his class was able to connect new content to previously learned material.

STRATEGY 23

Research Scavengers

Explanation

Students search for information related to a specific topic in pairs or small groups utilizing multiple resources.

Materials

- Variety of resources selected for references, possibly including the following:
  - Internet access, specific websites, texts, print media—newspapers, journals, magazines, and so on
  - Personal references

Advance Preparation

- Create research questions.
- Select groups.
- Create directions and graphic organizers as appropriate.
- Determine scavenger competition guidelines; that is, will students get a specific time (30 minutes) to complete hunt, or does first group done win, and so on.
- Ensure resources are available for students, including computers, the media room, and so on.

Directions

1. Select research topics and types of resources.
2. Place students in pairs or small groups.
3. Explain to the students that they will be participating in a fact-finding scavenger hunt and are required to use a number of resources, which they must cite when they respond to research questions.
4. Hand out individual folders or envelopes with scavenger information. Allow students to review directions and information together and walk around to make sure students understand directions and expectations. Groups may or may not have the same research information to address different needs.
5. Explain how much time students will have to work on the hunt and how they will be rewarded points (for correct answers or for time, etc.).
6. Explain hunting rules such as noise level, what areas in the classroom or school are fair play, and what to do if another group is using the resource they want.

7. When the groups are done, evaluate Research Scavenger completed assignments. Points may be assigned for correct responses and best time.
8. Have students share or post information with one another.
9. Announce hunt winners.

Sample Applications

English
- Questions for research papers, critiques of novels and plays, information for persuasive or expository essays

Math
- Research related to theorems, mathematicians, statistical data, and a variety of problem-solving activities, including word problems

Science
- Research questions on any topic of study such as geology, biology, environmental science; current science-related social issues

Social Studies
- Questions related to any topic of study such as historical figures, cultures and people, and current events.

Implementation Consideration

- Notify administration when you will be using this strategy, so there is no surprise when small groups of students are walking the halls; consider also notifying the librarian, media specialist, and other key people who need to know to expect students.
- This strategy is recommended as a cooperative learning experience typical to the scavenger hunt concept, so no one will feel alone or embarrassed in a competitive situation.

How This Strategy Can Support Individuals With Learning Differences

- Multiple entry points support different student functioning levels.
- Graphic organizers can be utilized to support individuals with metacognative issues.
- This strategy strengthens study and research skills.
- Movement and time expectations keep students motivated to remain on task.

Vignette Sample: Biology—Blood Functions

Mr. D. used Research Scavengers to promote research and meet learning objectives. He organized (or selected) groups and told students they would have to use both primary and secondary sources to respond to questions. Each group also had to use a variety of references: a personal source as a primary reference (doctor or patient with blood disorder) and secondary sources, including at least one website and one print media reference such as a magazine, journal, or news article.

He put students in groups of three and assigned them to one of three sets of questions according to ability: A, B, and C (see group questions below). There were three sets of research scavenger teams for every letter. Groups were allowed to use the entire class period. Mr. D. told them they could use the Internet on classroom computers and the library and media center, and they could speak to Mrs. L. in the cafeteria, Mr. B. himself, and Mrs. Z. in the main office as possible primary personal sources for specific interview questions.

Whoever finished first and had the most number of points for completed, accurate questions (five points each) won the group competition. An extra two points would be added if students had all answers correct and were the first group done.

Mr. D. used the Research Scavengers strategy on a day he had a 90-minute block for science. He spent only 15 minutes reviewing directions and allowing groups to review questions and create strategies together. He then let the students go. On the hour bell, students were directed to come back to class even if they weren't done with all the questions.

One group returned in 40 minutes, in a 55-minute period, with all questions accurately completed. The other groups returned five to six minutes prior to the bell, and together, the class reviewed responses, and Mr. D. evaluated references. Overall, the class enjoyed the responses, and the three winning teams had perfect scores with an extra two points for the fastest high scorer. That team earned an extra two points on the next exam. Any teams who did not get answers correct learned from those with correct answers. One interesting strategy was that one group actually e-mailed one of their mothers, who was a physician, as a primary resource, and she answered from her BlackBerry. Other personnel in the school were aware of the scavenger strategy and were excited to see the kids rushing to resources. Outside of a couple of "Slow downs" and "Remember to keep it quiets," the strategy was a highly motivating and productive learning experience that met diverse student needs.

Sample Research Scavenger Questions

Group A

Question	Answer	Resource (Indicate primary or secondary)
Identify blood types.		
Identify parts of blood and their functions.		
What are the most common blood diseases or disorders?		
Interview a person who treats blood disorders or a person with a blood disorder. From a doctor, find out about treatments for individuals with blood disorders and the most common types.		

Sample Research Scavenger Questions

Group B

Question	Answer	Resource
What is the color of blood? Explain why people think it is red.		
What are three careers related to working with blood, and how do you become qualified for such careers?		
Interview a person who treats blood disorders or a person with a blood disorder. From a doctor, find out about treatments for individuals with blood disorders and the most common types.		
Describe the roles of red and white blood platelets.		

Sample Research Scavenger Questions

Group C

Question	Answer	Resource
What are the three most common blood disorders and their symptoms and treatments?		
What are the major breakthroughs in medical science to help people with blood diseases?		
Interview a person who treats blood disorders or a person with a blood disorder. From a doctor, find out about treatments for individuals with blood disorders and the most common types.		

STRATEGY 24

Round Robin

Explanation

In this strategy, students brainstorm and share information about a topic. They rotate through stations, responding to questions and commenting on and adding to the contributions of others. At the end of the activity, students share information from the stations, and you facilitate a strong, student-centered discussion related to student responses.

Materials

- Large poster paper for the wall
- Tape
- Colored markers or pens

Advance Preparation

- Create four or five stations around the classroom by taping large poster paper to the wall or floor.
- Choose a different topic for each station, and develop material (questions, pictures, headlines, letters, etc.) for the students to respond to at each station.

Directions

1. Divide the class into the same number of groups as there are stations. Ask each group to stand at a station, and give them different-colored markers, so each group's contributions can be easily identified. This encourages accountability.
2. Groups work together to respond to the question at their station, and after a few minutes, students move to the next station.
3. At the next station, students add to the responses or make comments about the previous group's contributions.
4. At the end of the Round Robin activity, a student from each group shares the information from their last station.
5. You can then lead a discussion related to the station responses.

Sample Applications

English

- Characters and story lines: students share and develop descriptions or comparisons of characters and events in stories or novels, making text-to-text or text-to-self connections

Math
- Equations
- Word problems

Social Studies
- Questions related to any historical or current events topic
- Responses, including personal opinion, to a picture or headline from current events attached to the paper at each station

Science
- Questions related to any historical or current events topic

Implementation Considerations

- When designing your lesson, think about your station choices. Posters with colored markers are effective because it is easy to identify group responses, and poster paper acts as a visual focus for group discussion.
- When it is time for groups to move to the next station, transition signals such as lights or bells are helpful.
- Be sure to walk around and encourage all group members to participate.
- If you have five people in a group and five stations, you may ask students to rotate leaders within their groups as they move forward to new stations.
- Cooperative learning discussion takes place within and after station work.

How This Strategy Can Support Individuals With Learning Differences

- Written responses support students with auditory processing concerns.
- Students with higher aptitudes may respond more deeply or broadly to a subject.
- Group dynamic work and movement keeps student attention on task.

Vignette Sample: Social Studies—Civil Rights Movement

During a Social Studies class devoted to the American Civil Rights Movement, Mrs. D. decided to use the Round Robin strategy to help bring various elements about the Civil Rights Movement together in class discussion. First, she separated the class into five different groups, giving each a different-colored marker. Groups were selected with mixed-ability peers. Mrs. D. had five posters with different questions hung up around the room. She read the questions on the posters to the entire class. Questions included the following:

1. *Discuss key individuals and their contributions to the Civil Rights Movement.*
2. *Black Power meant different things to different people. Explain.*
3. *Describe the injustices to African Americans leading to the Civil Rights Movement.*
4. *Describe the injustices the Native Americans faced leading to the Civil Rights Movement.*
5. *Describe the injustices faced by Hispanics leading to the Civil Rights Movement.*

Groups were directed to stand in front of different posters, discuss the questions and possible solutions, and write responses. When Mrs. D. felt enough time had passed and students had made contributions, she signaled each group to move clockwise to the next poster. Mrs. D. explained groups could not repeat what another group wrote but should add or comment on it. As students moved to their fourth and fifth poster questions, it became more difficult to add something new. At this time, Mrs. D. allowed groups to use texts and notebooks as resources. When Mrs. D. called time, one person from each group read all poster responses. A wealth of knowledge was shared among the class. Question 1 answers were Malcolm X, Martin Luther King, Caesar Chavez, and Stokely Carmichael. The class had to discuss each person's contributions. Second question responses were these:

1. *Having black leadership*
2. *Sense of identity and pride in being black*
3. *Black is beautiful*
4. *A demand for civil, economic, and political rights for African Americans*
5. *Improved education and full employment*

Such responses led to rich discussions and elaborations. For a homework assignment, Mrs. D. asked students to select a poster question from the lesson to write an essay. Mrs. D. felt this strategy proved to be an excellent, student-centered, collaborative experience that supported the essay assignment. Sometimes, while sharing, students become uninterested in peer responses. Because everyone worked on every question, students were more interested in hearing their own group contributions announced and comparing other group input. Using colored markers helped Mrs. D. easily identify groupwork, making comments and probing further in discussion. This was a true, full-participation experience.

Resource

Jones, R. C. (2006). Carousel brainstorm. *Strategies for Reading Comprehension*. Winston-Salem, NC: Reading Quest. Retrieved from http://www.readingquest.org/strat/carousel.html

STRATEGY 25

Self-Reporting

Explanation

This strategy provides opportunities for students to self-evaluate and create action plans to support their own learning.

Materials

- Paper and pen

Advance Preparation

- Prepare a list of questions students need to answer to self-evaluate and improve performance. See sample below.

Directions

1. Determine when and what (content area, behavior, etc.) you'd like students to self-report about.
2. Ask students to complete the Self-Reporting template independently.
3. Ask students to share information from their reflections—volunteers only.
4. Ask students to review action plans for success, and remind them of the date they will be asked to self-report on action taken (typically no longer than one week, so students do not forget the task at hand).
5. Ask peers to brainstorm and offer support to their classmates when possible.

Sample Applications

English

- Student determines how well he or she develops essays and creates an action plan to improve performance by possibly including more perspective and related research to the topic or working on grammar and spelling.

Math

- Student determines if he or she needs more help in a specific area such as proofs or reviewing and memorizing multiplication and division of fraction rules.

Social Studies

- Student determines if he or she knows the causes and outcomes of the Civil War enough to pass an exam. Student creates a study action plan.

World Language

- Students determine if they can use new vocabulary or conjugate verbs appropriately in written language.

Behavior/Organization

- Student assesses his or her performance in being prepared, participating appropriately, or submitting homework regularly and completely.

Implementation Considerations

- Determine which issue you would like students to self-report about. It can be one concept in learning or midterm or final progress in a marking period.
- Students may write open-ended letters to themselves or complete the template to provide direction and clarity for other students.
- Determine how the information reported will be saved and used again. It is imperative to refer back to self-reporting as students monitor progress regularly to track goal setting, problem-solving skills, and personal growth.

How This Strategy Supports Individuals With Learning Differences

- Self-monitoring is an important component for motivating students and improving performance. This strategy provides an opportunity for students to reflect, self-assess, and organize strategies to improve performance.
- This strategy supports students with difficulties in attention, focus, and organization. It especially supports adolescents who have need of support in organization and are beginning to create their own self-identities. Reflection and goal setting are important critical-thinking skills to foster as students become young adults.
- Students with metacognitive needs can use this reflective, think-aloud-type strategy to identify and address problems with goals and an action plan.
- Students who prefer intrapersonal learning experiences can benefit from this strategy because it is self-reflective and provides no pressure to share with others, so students can self-report honestly without the pressure of being judged by peers.

Vignette Sample: World Language

Mr. F. was preparing to calculate progress report grades in the middle of the marking period. To help him evaluate student performance, he asked students to self-report. He gave them a small lecture on why it is important to sometimes stop and think about your own performance rather than wait to hear about it from someone else. He explained that the people in charge of their futures as young adults were the students themselves. Setting goals and making plans for success is a key life skill. Students could begin with specific goals, like success in a subject area.

Mr. F. asked students to self-reflect and identify their strengths and needs in his Spanish class as they moved toward the end of the school year. He handed out the Self-reporting

(Continued)

(Continued)

template and asked students to work independently. On the board, he wrote some of the key objectives for the term students might assess during reflections:

Masculine and feminine agreement

Conjugating regular and irregular verbs

Creating simple and complex sentences

New vocabulary

He told students no one had to share their responses with the class unless they wanted to, so they should be as honest as possible. When the class finished, he asked students to share information voluntarily. He learned many students still had trouble memorizing irregular verb conjugations. Most felt comfortable with regular verbs and masculine and feminine agreement. When asked to identify different ways students would support their learning, students' answers included study more, make flash cards, and go to peer tutoring. Mr. F. was so impressed with the avid response to this assignment that he set up Thursdays as afterschool help days for students needing extra support. He then told students to put their goals in class folders and be ready to reevaluate in one month. Students who could identify problems without solutions were able to listen to what their classmates contributed and use some of those examples to create strategies for personal success.

An example of a student-completed template is below.

Goals

Name ______________________________ **Date** ______________________________

At this time, I believe my performance studying ____*Spanish*____ can be Rated ___*3*___ (1–5, with 1 being the lowest and 5 being the highest).

I understand about

Feminine and masculine
Changing regular verbs

I can use more help understanding

New vocabulary
Conjugating irregular verbs

I think I don't understand because

I don't study enough
I don't memorize the new verbs

To support my learning I can

Put time aside to study

Work after school with my teacher

I plan to complete my action plan by

Studying more

I will self-report again

May 22

Goals

Name ______________________ **Date** ______________________

At this time I believe my performance studying ________________ can be rated __________ (1–5, with 1 being the lowest and 5 being the highest).

I understand about

I can use more help understanding

I think I don't understand because

To support my learning I can

I plan to complete my action plan by

I will self-report again

STRATEGY 26

Spiderweb

Explanation

The Spiderweb is an interactive activity that has a variety of uses and has a strong focus on content. Students stand in a circle and toss a ball of yarn from student to student, creating a spiderweb of colorful yarn. As each student catches the ball of yarn, she has to respond to the question that the teacher has posed.

Materials

- A large ball of yarn
- A pair of scissors

Directions

1. Decide on the content area and develop one open-ended question to ask the students.
2. Ask students to stand in a circle. Hold the ball of yarn in one hand, and the loose end of the ball of yarn in the other hand.
3. Pose the question to the students, look around to see who indicates readiness to answer, and then throw the ball of yarn to that person while holding on to the loose end tightly. Holding on to the tail end of the yarn is key here.
4. The student who catches the yarn has to answer the question and throw the ball to a classmate across from him or her, while holding on to the tail end of the yarn. The second person responds to the same question and then throws the ball of yarn, and so on, until everyone has had a turn.
5. As the ball of yarn is thrown from one student to the next, a spiderweb is created, and each student is holding a piece of it. At the same time as the web is being created, information is being shared about the topic or content area.

Sample Applications

Literature

- What do you feel was the most compelling theme or message in the most recent piece of literature we read as a class?
- Who is your favorite author, and why?
- Considering all of the literature we have examined so far this semester, what stylistic element do you feel has been the most successful?

World Language

- Use the target language for both the question stem and student responses.

Math

- At the end of the semester, identify one topic we covered in class and explain how it relates to the job market.

Suitable for a Variety of Subject Areas

- Of all of the people we have studied this year, or over the course of this unit, who has influenced you the most, and why (suitable for the end of a course in Art History, Philosophy, Psychology, Literature, Poetry, etc.)?
- What is one thing you learned from this course (or this unit) that was most interesting to you?
- What is one thing you learned from this course (or this unit) that you are able to apply to real life, either now or in the future?
- What topic that we have covered in this course do you feel most competent to teach others, and why?
- Choose one piece of popular media (a movie, a song, a commercial, etc.) that relates to the subject matter in this course, and explain why.
- Describe a current news story (it can be local, national, or worldwide).

Implementation Considerations

Grouping

- This is most effective as a whole group strategy with the teacher as facilitator.

Timing

- The objective of the strategy dictates the amount of time needed. The Spiderweb can be used fairly quickly at the end of the lesson as a review, or it can be used as a review at the end of a longer unit or as a substantial piece of the lesson itself, depending on both the content and the question posed. This also works as an end-of-course review.
- Using the Spiderweb with a more in-depth question or sentence stem and pairing it with asking students to write about it in their journals as a follow-up should easily take the whole class period.

How This Strategy Can Support Individuals With Learning Differences

- The Spiderweb can support individuals with attention issues because of the opportunity for movement for a specific purpose and because of the novelty of the strategy (the appeal of something different). Typically, middle and high school students spend a large portion of their days in their seats, and research shows the benefit that moving has on learning, engagement, and retention.
- The open-ended nature of the questions encourages higher-order thinking and allows for creativity.
- Students can self-select when to take their turns; this supports the individual who needs additional time to process the question and to formulate an answer.

- This strategy showcases individual strengths.
- Some students find it easier to express themselves verbally as opposed to in writing.

Vignette Sample: Literature

Mr. M.'s class read several contemporary novels that reflect Southern culture, including Fried Green Tomatoes, Cold Sassy Tree, The Secret Life of Bees, *and* The Color Purple. *As a culminating lesson, he decided to use the Spiderweb. He had the class stand in a circle, gave directions, and posed the following question: "Thinking back on the novels we read that reflect Southern culture, what was the most compelling theme, message, or character, either from one or more of the books or from all of the books that we have read collectively." He gave the class a moment to consider the question, and then caught Angela's eye, who indicated that she was ready to answer.*

Mr. M. held on to the tail end of the yarn and threw the ball of yarn to Angela, who caught it easily and gave a thoughtful answer. She held on to her piece of yarn and threw the ball to the next student, who answered and continued the chain. The question got answered, many different opinions and points of view were voiced, and a variety of themes emerged, complete with supporting details. As the answers flowed, the yarn continued to be passed from one student to the next (most often between students across the room from each other), and a Spiderweb of yarn was created in the circle. Students elaborated on their answers, and the web took most of the period to complete.

As the students filed out the door, chattering, Mr. M. reflected on the strategy. In addition to the thoughtful responses, he was most pleased that every class member had something to share—all good ideas—which is something that did not happen frequently enough in more traditional class discussions.

STRATEGY 27

Teacher–Teacher

Explanation

Students use a reciprocal teaching approach to review and reinforce learning by creating and implementing their own lesson plans for a peer.

Materials

- Lesson Plan template
- Manipulatives as needed

Advance Preparation

- You must model how to develop a lesson plan using the template and do one example with the class together.

Directions

1. Introduce the Lesson Plan template to the class and complete one example to model instructions.
2. Ask the students to write brief lesson plans using the template to teach a concept to a peer.
3. Tell the class what the concept and learning objective are. Every student has the same learning objective.
4. After students complete their individual lesson plans using any resources needed, such as texts and notes, assign everyone a peer to teach the lesson to.
5. After each pair teaches to one another, the students can be assigned another peer to work with or may just hand in the Lesson Plan template with an evaluation of peer performance.

Sample Applications

Math

- Teach any concept: identifying mean, median, or mode; finding the area or volume of figures; finding proofs for different geometry problems; graphing; and so on.

Science

- Teach any concept such as chemistry or physics formulas and problems.

Social Studies

- Teach about a period in history, such as explaining the life of lords and serfs, discussing communism in China, or explaining how the League of Nations was formed.

Language Arts
- ○ Teach rules of grammar, such as use of commas and semicolons, editing, or proofreading.

World Language
- ○ Teach rules of grammar, such as how to conjugate verbs, or how to use new vocabulary successfully in sentences.

Implementation Considerations

- Every pair can be given the same concept, or you can choose to differentiate and give some pairs higher-level objectives as appropriate. In either case, each member of a pair has the same objective that he or she will teach the other.
- Once students are finished teaching a concept to a peer, the peer teaches the same concept in return. Choosing to do the same concept allows more rehearsal for practice and retrieval, even when a student has mastered the concept. It also provides a nonthreatening opportunity and a greater chance of success for lower-performing students to succeed in a cooperative learning situation.
- Ask students to be creative in explanations, and allow students to use manipulatitves, graphs, calculators, maps, text excerpts, and so on, as part of the learning procedures.
- Use submitted student lessons, evaluations, and work samples to assess student progress and make future lesson decisions.

How This Strategy Can Support Individuals With Learning Differences

- Reciprocal teaching is one of the best ways you can identify if a student has mastered a concept. Allowing students to reciprocal teach to their peers helps to review, rehearse, and reinforce concepts.
- This strategy supports individuals with metacognitive issues as they identify and practice steps with one specific concept.
- The strategy can have multiple entry points for students with different functioning levels.
- This strategy provides an opportunity for students with language needs to practice communication skills in a one-on-one peer experience.
- Students benefit from hearing an explanation from another student rather than always from the teacher; students can come up with different approaches to share, which the teachers may not have thought of. Another approach and voice may resonate with the learner.

Vignette Sample: Math—Factoring Polynomials

On Tuesday, Mr. G. discussed the test that the class would take on Friday. He explained the test would be on multiplying and factoring polynomials. He reviewed both multiplying and factoring concepts with the class and did a couple of examples each at the board. He asked the class if there were any questions. When no one raised a hand, he told the class

(Continued)

(Continued)

they must really understand the concept, so to review, the students were now going to assume the role of teacher and teach it.

Most of the class didn't understand what he was talking about, as Sima said, "What," and Jason said, "To who?" Then, Mr. G. said, "I am passing out lesson forms that you are each expected to complete and use with a peer." "Oh, good!" Steven said with a sigh of relief. After Mr. G. handed out the Lesson Plan templates, he put one on his SMART Board and modeled how to complete a lesson plan for factoring polynomials.

Lesson Objective (What concept are you teaching?)

Factoring polynomials

Procedure

- Prepare directions and explanation for the student
- You can use a chart, manipulatives, and so on

Step 1: Identify the GCF of the polynomial.

Remember: the GCF is the largest monomial that divides (or can be factored) into each term.

Step 2: Divide the GCF out of every term of the polynomial.

Practice example(s) with teacher assistance

$14y^5 - 4y^3 + 2y$

The GCF is the number 2

$14y^5 - 4y^3 + 2y$
$2y(7y^4 - 2y^2 + 1)$

Practice example(s) without the teacher

$15x^4 - 9x + 3x^1$

Evaluation (Was the lesson a success? Explain.)

After removing the information from the SMART Board, Mr. G. told the class to begin writing a lesson plan using the template he distributed. Several students called out, "But you just did it!" "That's OK," quieted Mr. G. "It's your turn to be the teacher. See if you can write the steps and examples. You may refer to your notes or the text if necessary." The students worked busily. Mr. G. helped students who needed it as he walked around the room.

When it appeared all the students were done, Mr. G. asked them to teach the concept to a neighboring student, each taking a turn as teacher and student. In closure, students shared how well their performances were as teachers. Most said they did good jobs and their students learned. Mr. G. asked if there were any students who thought their teachers didn't do good jobs. Jason raised his hand and said, "My teacher didn't give me enough time to finish!" Sima said, "My teacher did the whole problem for me." Mr. G. said, "Who had good luck?" Mary said, "Sima was patient and explained it well." Mr. G. also asked if students believed they could factor polynomials more confidently. A majority replied yes. Mr. G. asked that all students put their names on the papers and hand them forward before leaving.

This strategy helped students review steps for factoring polynomials several times. Each worked with Mr. G. independently, and with a peer in the role of student and teacher. Instead of just saying "Study," Mr. G. created an active learning experience with repetition and engagement to help students review. By collecting and reviewing student work, Mr. G. has a better understanding of who has mastered the concepts and who needs more help.

Lesson Plan Template

Lesson Objective (What concept are you teaching?)

Procedure

- Prepare directions and explanation for the student
- You can use a chart, manipulatives, and so on

Practice example(s) with teacher assistance

Practice example(s) without the teacher

Evaluation (Was the lesson a success? Explain.)

STRATEGY 28

Text Message

Explanation

Students, assuming the role of someone they are learning about or working together to solve a problem, write and respond to text messages from one another. Text messages are shared with a Text Message template instead of cell phones.

Materials

- Paper and pen

or

- Text template (see below)

Advance Preparation

- Determine what information will be shared in text messages. For example, create a list of identities that are meaningful to the learning concept you are teaching; then select word problems or beginning statements, that is, "To factor polynomials, you . . ."
- Select students who will work together if random grouping is not appropriate.
- Create handouts that have the texting directions at the top.

Directions

1. Select information to be shared among students.
2. Provide students with handouts of directions for how they should begin texting and what or who they are working on. Students can write messages with up to 120 characters.
3. When students are ready, have them pass on the Text Message to a peer.
4. The student who reads the passed text then replies with an appropriate response.
5. The student then passes the text to another peer in the group.
6. The text continues to move on until the teacher calls time.
7. The students then share texts aloud in groups or with the entire class.

Sample Applications

English
- Text messages to different characters in literature

Social Studies

- Text messages to different individuals in history, such as emperors and local people, crusaders, presidents, and so on

Science

- Text messages used to solve different problems—for example, in Chemistry—using the solubility rules, predict what will happen when the following solutions are mixed: $KNO_3(aq)$ and BaCL(aq) (student may begin to find the solution and pass on a text, or if it is solved, the next student can comment on the accuracy of the answer)

Math

- Text messages used to solve word problems or equations—for example, in Calculus—find the derivative of $f(x) = x^2 + 3x$ (in this case, students can choose to solve and interpret)

World Language

- Text messages can be on any topic or just social communication among one another in another language—for example—"Discuss your weekend plans in French with your peers"

Implementation Considerations

- Determine what will work best: purposeful or random grouping. Decide who will text whom. Will texting be a random pass to different peers, or will students only text back and forth to selected partners?
- Provide the whole class with multiple names or problems to solve, or give all students the same directions.
- Do one sample together with the class to model the strategy before all participate.
- Differentiate by providing specific topics and problems for different functioning levels.
- Allow students to refer to texts or other resources as needed.

How This Strategy Can Support Individuals With Learning Differences

- Students with auditory processing concerns are supported with visual supports.
- Activity keeps individuals with attention deficits active and interested in new and novel responses.
- Higher-aptitude learners can have different text information to match skill levels.
- This strategy supports comprehension and retention as students practice or apply information.
- To support individuals with metacognitive concerns, begin the first message for them.
- As with real texting, grammar is not a priority; the content is important. This should support students who are anxious about writing skills.

Vignette Sample: English Literature—*Hamlet*

After reading the first act of Hamlet, *Mrs. G. used the Text Message strategy to support comprehension and predictions for further reading. She placed students in random groups of five, each with specific directions:*

Student 1: Horatio begins to text with Hamlet.

Student 2: Prince Hamlet texts to his mother Gertrude.

Student 3: Queen Gertrude texts to King Claudius.

Student 4: Polonius texts to Ophelia.

Student 5: Wildcard—Begin a texting between any characters.

After five minutes of texting, the teacher asked the class to rotate the text papers clockwise through their group. As students received new texts, they read and responded as the character assigned. The papers passed to all five students, and Mrs. G. had the students share among themselves. Students in each group were very eager to hear how the texts progressed because each student only wrote one response. There was a lot of laughter and chatter as students shared with one another. Then, Mrs. G. asked students in Groups 1 and 2 to choose one text message to share with the class.

Mrs. G. asked if the class had similar responses and if the information in the text messages was based on accurate information from the play. Students shared comments, and Mrs. G. asked students to refer to the text to support their responses as needed.

The experience made the students excited to share and more motivated to read the next act of a play, which was not one of their favorites the week before!

Text Between Horatio and Hamlet

Horatio:	OMG! U should have seen ur dads ghost last night at the castle! He nos who killed him. It freaked me out!
Prince Hamlet:	r u crazy?!?! Were u hallucinating?
Horatio:	for real! Ur dads ghost told me it was ur uncle who killed him so he could get the throne.
Prince Hamlet:	I believe it u hav to help me kill Claudius. Meet me @ the moat to at 10 am to make a plan.
Horatio:	kk but u owe me big-time!

TEXT TEMPLATE

Message from: ____

Message to: ____

Message from: ____

Message to: ____

STRATEGY 29

Theme Boards

Explanation

A theme is a "distinct, recurring, and unifying quality or idea" (Microsoft Encarta Dictionary).

In this strategy, students work in small groups to explore the underlying themes or key ideas in a given unit of study and create a poster board that in some way reflects these themes.

Materials

- Poster boards or computer paper
- Fine-tipped magic marker
- Sticky notes (different colors or sizes work well)

Advance Preparation

- Plan lesson content.

Directions

1. Remind students what a theme is. Talk about what themes are, where they are found, and why they are important. (Perhaps a brief review here is all that is needed, depending on prior knowledge, student level, or areas of study.)
2. Explain to students that, as you are teaching the lesson, discussing the topic, or reading the novel, their job is to be on the lookout for recurring themes. They will be looking for recurring themes, specific examples of each, and what the meanings are.
3. During the lesson, encourage students to write down notes on sticky notes, one sticky note per item. If you so choose, you can stop every 10 or 15 minutes to give students two minutes to write.
4. Instruct them to put sticky notes on the board. Have students work in groups of three or four to discuss what they each have written, moving the sticky notes around until they have found like themes that can be grouped together.
5. Students use the grouped sticky notes to create posters in any way that they see fit that reflects what they have determined are the key themes for this area of study.
6. Finished products can be used as a springboard for essay writing, PowerPoint presentations, or expository speech.

Sample Applications

English
- Novels (e.g., *Night, The House on Mango Street*)
- Poetry (e.g., Langston Hughes, Tupac Shakur)
- Drama (e.g., "Brighton Beach Memoirs")

History
- Expansion (imperialism)
- Human rights (enfranchisement)
- Conflict and compromise (civil rights)

Science
- Habitats
- Health and nutrition
- Technology

Implementation Considerations

- Depending on the level of your class and individual needs, you can work as a whole group to create a list that identifies and describes key themes at the beginning of the lesson. This gives students the advantage of knowing what they are looking for.
- Once students are familiar with this strategy, it can be incorporated easily into many different lessons.

How This Strategy Can Support Individuals With Learning Differences

- Students know exactly what they need to focus on and listen for during the lesson.
- This strategy works well for all learners as each student can participate at his or her own level.
- This strategy supports metacognition.
- Moving sticky notes to group together like ideas lends a tangible element to a more abstract discussion and helps students to see how ideas fit together.
- The completed poster becomes a visual reference for the subject matter.

Vignette Sample: English

Mr. T.'s high school class was working on résumé writing. He spent a fair amount of time introducing the subject. He started by talking about what a résumé is supposed to accomplish and then invited the school principal to come into class to talk about what she looked for when reading a résumé. He followed this up by visits from other people who regularly read résumés, including the parent of one of the students in the class. Some of the visits were in person, and others were virtual visits using available technology, and some of the visitors provided sample résumés for the students to look at. Each visit was fairly short but gave the class the opportunity to hear about the importance of résumés firsthand.

(Continued)

(Continued)

Next, Mr. T. gave students an article to read that focused on the purpose of a résumé, and then he provided the class with a résumé template suitable for someone just entering the job market.

Throughout these lessons, a number of themes emerged centering on the purpose—the art and the craft of constructing a résumé. Mr. T. wanted his students to think about what they had learned, to date, and synthesize all of the information into themes that needed to be taken into consideration when writing a résumé.

He let the class pick their own groups and provided lots of sticky notes of varying colors and sizes and a poster board for each group. Members of each group each wrote down on the sticky notes what they felt to be important and then put them randomly on the poster board. That was when the fun began. Each group read all of the sticky notes on their boards and started to discuss some of the similarities and differences, and through this discussion, a few very distinct themes emerged.

One of the common themes that Mr. T. was happy to see was the importance of how the résumé looked, including writing, grammar, spelling, and even addressing it to the correct person. When each group had a few common themes, they wrote each of those themes on their poster boards and then put each sticky note under the theme it represented. (Thus, the sticky notes for "correct grammar," "correct spelling," "look neat," "use legible font," and "make sure you have the correct name and spelling of who you are sending it to" were each put under the theme of How the Résumé Looks to the Person Reading It.)

When the poster boards where complete, the class had several visual references that they had designed to remind everyone of the important points to keep in mind when constructing a résumé. Mr. T. felt that having the students come up with the common themes underscored the importance of what they learned.

When he was ready to have students write their own résumés, he followed a similar process. This time working individually, students were once again given sticky notes and poster boards and told to write down, one point on each note, what they thought they wanted to include in their résumés. After this step was completed, they were given the résumé template again and worked to arrange their sticky notes on poster boards to fit into the template design. This prompted a lot of discussion and helped students to decide which facts to eliminate and which areas to strengthen.

STRATEGY 30

Through Our Own Lens

Explanation

As part of a unit of study, students work individually to examine or research the topic in a way that it relates to them.

Materials

- Resources on the topic in the classroom or the library
- List of relevant websites

Advance Preparation

- Consider in advance which criterion is most appropriate for your topic.

Directions

1. Start with content in mind.
2. Explain that you are going to continue your study of ____________ but with a twist. Each student will be charged with researching information about the content area individually. Depending on the subject matter, ask students to examine the content as it relates to one of the following criteria: people their own age, birthplace of their grandparents, country where they (or their parents) were born, gender, or socioeconomic class. You will choose the "lens" that students will use.
3. Give students an example of how this strategy works: If the content topic is Ellis Island and the Statue of Liberty, for example, explain that students would start by identifying their heritage; they will then be charged with tracing their families' paths to immigrate to the United States.
4. The time frame for this strategy varies according to content and time available. When students have finished their research, they come together as a class for a discussion. Each student shares (briefly), while you note on a chart the key point(s) that each student has contributed to the topic. Students can fill out the same chart at their seats. This chart varies according to the topic and the "lens." (One difference, for example, could be the number of different experiences included. The content headings in each box might be another change.)

Variations

- When individual research is completed, each student can present a three- to five-slide PowerPoint to the class instead of having a class discussion.

- Instead of filling in a chart, students can take the information they learn from classmates and make a collage or a poster, individually or in small groups.
- Students from similar backgrounds, for example, can choose to work together. Even if they work separately, they can share together, and one box on the chart can represent all five of those students, for example.

Sample Applications

English

- When reading *To Kill a Mockingbird* and discussing the "treasures" hidden in a tree by Jem, Scout, and Dill, ask students to bring "treasures" from their own lives and to choose containers of special significance to carry them; students will explain the significance of their "treasures" to classmates.

Social Studies

- What was the role of men (or of women) in WWII?
- We are studying the different decades in the 1900s in the United States. Interview a family member of your choice who was born during this time—ask him or her to choose one decade in U.S. history that he or she lived through and tell you the highlights that he or she remembers.
- Research the election process in your country of origin. How does it differ from that of the United States?

Economics

- What is the current economic system of the country in which your grandparents (or great-grandparents) were born? How does it differ from that of the United States? What currency did they use historically? What currency do they use today, and how does it correlate with the dollar?

Science

- Research a famous scientist from the country that your ancestors were from.
- Research the vegetation and animal life indigenous to the country that your ancestors were from.

Math

- Choose a state that you have a personal connection to, that is, where your parents were born, that you have visited, or where you are considering applying to college, and so on. Let students research whatever the topic is in terms of how it relates to that particular state. This lends itself well to the study of percentages or statistics and comparison (unemployment, demographics, weather, size, distance).

Implementation Considerations

- This is a strategy in which students work individually.
- Time frame is flexible and can be varied as you see fit. Some of the work may be assigned to do for homework or as a longer-term project.

How This Strategy Can Support Individuals With Learning Differences

- Students work individually at their own level and at their own pace.
- This strategy allows students to make personal connections to the content, which has the potential to increase motivation and make learning more meaningful. This is particularly important for the reluctant learner.
- Adolescent learners appreciate choice, and in this strategy, each student has a say in what the research focus will be.
- Some students will benefit from an example of your expectations.
- The chart helps students to keep on task and provides a focus as to what to listen for during the peer presentations.

Vignette Sample: Social Studies and American History

Mrs. R.'s high school class was studying WWII. She wanted her students to take a personal interest and to understand the many ramifications of the war. To start off the unit, she spent the first few class periods giving the class background information about the war.

In the next lesson, she had each student indentify a country that his or her ancestors were from. The students were charged with researching the role of that county in the war and how that country was affected by WWII. Mrs. R. provided resources at a variety of reading levels and gave students lists of relevant websites as well.

José, a recent immigrant from El Salvador, chose to research El Salvador's role in the war. At first, his findings disappointed him. El Salvador had not joined the war on the side of the Allies until late in the war. Being a young man with a strong sense of ethics, he had hoped that "his country" had quickly joined in the fight to help the victims of oppression and hatred in Europe. Upon further investigation he found the story of an El Salvadorian Oscar Schindler. José Castellanos, an army colonel and diplomat, helped save 25,000 European Jews. Mrs. R.'s student's pride was exhibited in the PowerPoint slide show he made and presented not only to his class but to guests in the classroom. From that point on, he began to research El Salvador's role in other world events, always coming to class eager to announce what he had learned.

(More info on José Castellanos can be found at http://www.guardian.co.uk/world/2008/jun/19/secondworldwar.)

Mrs. R. found that all of her students were more motivated to do this research and eagerly took part in the class discussion that ensued.

Source: This vignette is based on a unit taught by Mrs. Judi Ricucci, a New Jersey high school special education teacher.

Template for a 25-Student Class

Student 1 Country:__________	Student 2 Country:__________	Student 3 Country:__________	Student 4 Country:__________	Student 5 Country:__________
Student 6 Country:__________	Student 7 Country:__________	Student 8 Country:__________	Student 9 Country:__________	Student 10 Country:__________
Students 11, 12, 13, and 14 Country:__________				
Student 16 Country:__________	Student 17 Country:__________	Student 18 Country:__________	Student 19 Country:__________	Student 20 Country:__________
Student 21 Country:__________	Student 22 Country:__________	Students 23 and 24 Country:__________		Student 25 Country:__________

STRATEGY 31

Traveling Teams

Explanation

In this strategy, students rotate with one another, meeting and speaking with peers to gain information and make decisions (similar to the speed dating concept).

Materials

- Topics or questions to be discussed
- Paper and pen

Advance Preparation

- You may decide to make a Q&A sheet or an informational graphic organizer (see sample).
- You should think about best groupings to ensure students feel secure in sharing with one another. Consider social needs and ability levels, so students can support one another.

Directions

1. Determine which topics you'd like to have students share.
2. Pair students, and provide each pair with the same list of questions or problems to solve. See sample.
3. Tell the class they have five to 10 minutes to address as many of the questions on the worksheet as possible, recording their responses.
4. Ask pairs to stand up with papers and pens in hand and match up with another pair. There should be four students now working together.
5. Pairs, now in groups of four, compare notes and add or change information from their sheets as necessary.
6. Students work in groups of four for three to five minutes until you signal them to stop.
7. Then, each pair leaves the group and finds a new pair to work with for another three to five minutes.
8. Each time new pairs meet in groups, they share and build information from their sheets.
9. At the end of the experience, students are asked about the product and the process of this strategy. First, ask them to share information learned. Second, ask them to identify how the process may or may not have been helpful, identifying the pros and cons of cooperative learning with their peers.

Sample Applications

Math

- Word problems, having students solve as many as they can together as they move from group to group

Science

- Questions related to any science topic, such as energy, chemical reactions, atomic theory, and so on

Social Studies

- Questions related to significant people and places

Language Arts

- Literature
- Questions about character, plot, and other parts of stories and novels
- Building on creative writing pieces from one group to another

World Language

- Student questions about themselves or specific topics to promote conversation and practice speaking another language

Implementation Considerations

- Consider providing roles for students, such as scribe and discussant.
- Students can work on material as a review or construct new material together with resources.
- Students may also be asked to review study materials and questions for homework in preparation for the Traveling Teams strategy.

How This Strategy Can Support Individuals With Learning Differences

- This quick-paced strategy appeals to the adolescent learner who is sometimes easily embarrassed or who may have academic or social issues. This strategy uses speed to create a fast-paced, fun experience and allows students to work in groups to encourage participation and create a sense of security among each other.
- This strategy supports individuals with social issues as it provides opportunities to work cooperatively and share in pairs or small groups with a purpose.
- Students may be assigned different names or concepts based on ability.
- The products from this strategy can be used as a study guide to support skills.
- This strategy supports students' attention deficits as it is a fast-paced learning experience with movement.

Vignette Sample: Social Studies—The Age of Revolution

In a Social Studies class, students were studying the Age of Revolution. Students were tasked: Define revolution, *and share information about the Industrial Revolution, Science Revolution, French Revolution, and Russian Revolution. On a handout, Mrs. H. wrote the headers: Dates—Causes, Significant People and Events, and Outcomes. Mrs. H. decided to pair students so that four students were working at one time, two pairs together. Each pair had one handout. After reviewing the definition of* revolution*—a change in power or organizational structure that takes place in a relatively short period of time—Mrs. H. called the partners' names she'd carefully selected by connecting students who she felt complemented one another's social and academic needs. Each pair had five to seven minutes to respond to the handout using classroom resources such as texts and computers. Then, student pairs were designated as movers. Each moving pair was directed to begin working with the group to the right of them. When the signal sounded (a bell), they had to stop and go on to the next pair to the right. When the bell sounded again, students could ask as many questions as they could related to the handout questions to develop their handouts with as much detail as possible related to the first topic, the Industrial Revolution. Students chatted by asking questions to one another and jotting down information. As with speed dating, there was very limited time to share, so students had to speak and jot down information as fast as they could. When the bell sounded again, the movers moved to the next group on the right and discussed the second topic, the Science Revolution. This process continued until each of the moving groups had met with four different pairs.*

When every pair rotated four times, addressing each of the topics, Mrs. H. asked students to share information. Some students identified Galileo as one of the significant people from the Science Revolution, and all students had Napoleon Bonaparte and the Reign of Terror listed under the significant names and events in the French Revolution. When asked to discuss the process of learning during the day's lesson, students said they really enjoyed it. One even said it would be better if they assigned one person the writer and one the orator, even rotating for each group, to save time.

The Age of Revolution

Student Names

____

____

Revolution: a change in power or organizational structure that takes place in a relatively short period of time.

Science Revolution	Industrial Revolution
French Revolution	Russian Revolution

For each revolution, share and develop information related to the following:

Dates

Causes

Significant People

Significant Events

Outcomes

STRATEGY 32

True or False

Explanation

Each student is handed an index card with a statement about the lesson content and has to use research to decide if the statement is True or False. Students determine the authenticity of each statement based on their readings.

Materials

- A wide variety of materials on the topic—some suggested types are articles, web addresses, books, class texts, videotaped interviews, famous speeches on tape, and so on (materials should represent a range of reading levels)
- Large index cards, at least one per student

Advance Preparation

- Write a list of statements about your topic, enough for one per student. Approximately half of these should be true, and the other half should be false.
- List one statement at the top of each index card.

Directions

1. Give each student one of the index cards you have prepared. Direct students to determine if their statements are True or False using any of the materials available to research their answers.

2. Students have to add information to the index cards that supports their votes and then put the cards in either the true pile or the false pile.

3. When students are finished, reconvene as a class. You will start the discussion about the topic, using each card as a talking point. You might want to number the cards so that the information and discussion unfold sequentially if appropriate.

Variations

- This can be used as a chapter, unit, or end-of-the-year review, and students can have time to reread their notes and refer to the course text.
- As a review, have the class work in groups to make up the statement cards, half true and half false. Then, redistribute the cards among the different groups. (Students are responsible for an answer key for each card they write.)
- Type up a list of all of the statements, with space next to each one for students to take notes. After the research has been completed and students

have finished their individual index cards, make the list available, either in paper form or electronically, so students have a template to take notes during the sharing portion of the lesson. (See the template example.)

Sample Applications

Health
- The effect of tobacco on the body

Math
- The stock market
- Probability

Economics
- The concept of supply and demand

Science
- Endangered river turtles
- Einstein's theory of relativity
- Famous scientists: Marie Curie, Isaac Newton, Albert Einstein, or Lewis Howard Latimer
- The characteristics of chemical changes

Implementation Considerations

- In our experience, it is more difficult to write false statements that do not sound obvious. This could be a good strategy to prepare with a coteacher or another member of your department.
- Giving each student in the class one statement may be inefficient for a variety of reasons, time being a primary concern. In this case, you can either have the students work in pairs, so half as many statements need to be written and discussed, or you can give each student his or her own index card to research independently but double up on the facts so that two students each get the same fact to research. Sharing 12 facts takes less time than discussing 24 and may fit better into the available time frame while still accomplishing the learning objectives for that lesson.

How This Strategy Can Support Individuals With Learning Differences

- Students can work in pairs.
- You can provide an assortment of reading and research materials and web addresses that represent a variety of reading levels. If the class text is too difficult for some, for example, you can make available library books, articles, and web addresses that might be more on target for lower-level readers. Interviews on tape and video clips from news stories are other valid sources of information. Students are free to use whatever materials they choose, but you can guide student choices according to reading level, content, and interest. This is an effective way to differentiate the lesson by

resource while still expecting each student to do some research and keeping your learning objectives the same for everyone.

- Researching individual facts provides students with practice using resources to find out information. This can serve as an informal assessment of beginning research skills.
- Providing a range of reading and research materials and offering students the choice as to what to use seamlessly differentiates for reading ability and visual perceptual issues.
- Providing the time up front to do the research before students have to answer gives needed time for the child who may process information more slowly and benefits from additional time to develop and formulate an answer. This supports a student with communication issues.
- Using this strategy to introduce a topic can be a way to generate interest and helps students to develop their own questions about the material to be covered.
- The structure of the strategy lends itself to developing a study guide that students can fill out themselves as they listen to student responses.

Source: Silberman, M. (1996). *Active learning: 101 strategies to teach any subject.* Needham Heights, MA: Allyn & Bacon.

Vignette Sample: Humanities, English, Social Studies, Music, and the Arts

Ms. O.'s class was studying Austria. To introduce the unit, she made up one index card per student. Half of the index cards had true facts about Austria, and the other half of the statements were false. She explained to the students that it was their job was to utilize any of the materials she had assembled in the classroom, including books, travel books, the course text, a world map, and web addresses, to decide if the statements were True or False.

She included the following true statements:

Mozart was born in Salzburg, Austria, and moved to Vienna to write his music.

Austria was once connected to Hungary.

WWI began with the assassination of Archduke Franz Ferdinand, who was the heir to the Austro-Hungarian throne.

The original story of the Sound of Music *took place in Austria.*

A few of the false statements she wrote on index cards were the following:

Beethoven was born in Salzburg, Austria.

Vienna is the main seaport of Austria.

Austria has the lowest standard of living in Europe today.

Austria is bordered by the Czech Republic, Germany, France, and Spain.

She gave the class some time to research the validity of their statements. When they found the answers, they were directed to write the word true *or* false *on the flip side of the index cards and to add one to three facts from their research that supported why it was either True or False.*

(Continued)

(Continued)

When the students were finished, Ms. O. asked them what they had learned so far about Austria. She let each student read his or her statement and explain why it was True or False. Michael explained that Mozart was born in Salzburg, Austria, and moved to Vienna to write music (a true statement) and added that Austria, in general, and Vienna, specifically, made major contributions to music. Many famous composers made their homes there, and today, Vienna is filled with numerous opulent concert halls.

Andrea had a false statement that Beethoven was born in Salzburg, Austria. She explained that he was actually born in Germany but joined several other famous composers and musicians who made their homes in Vienna. Sebastian emphatically told the class that Vienna being the main seaport of Austria was clearly not true because Austria is landlocked.

Each student had the opportunity to read his or her answer with explanations and contribute to the growing body of knowledge the class was compiling about Austria. The result was a lesson that allowed each of the students to contribute information as opposed to a lesson where the teacher does all of the talking. Ms. O. liked the strategy and decided that, next time, after the students were finished with the research, she would hand out typed sheets of all of the statements, with space next to each for students to take notes as their classmates discussed each fact or nonfact. She also considered using available technology.

Template for Students to Take Notes

Facts	Notes
Mozart was born in Salzburg, Austria, and moved to Vienna to write his music. **TRUE** or **FALSE**	
Austria was once connected to Hungary. **TRUE** or **FALSE**	
Austria has the lowest standard of living in Europe today. **TRUE** or **FALSE**	
WWI began with the assassination of Archduke Franz Ferdinand, who was the heir to the Austro-Hungarian throne. **TRUE** or **FALSE**	

Note-Taking Template for True or False Strategy

Statement	True or False	Supporting Facts

Explanation

Students create a Wanted Poster describing a prominent figure or important concept they are learning about with a clever, related reward.

Materials

- Poster board and markers
- Pictures from the Internet
- Variety of resources for information

Advance Preparation

- Select information to be used for Wanted Poster. Information may be from material already learned, or it may be new concepts, and students bring newly constructed information into a student-centered cooperative learning experience.

Directions

1. Distribute information for students to complete wanted posters.
2. Students write a description, using facts, of their wanted person or concept. This is the basis for their posters.
3. Students create a clever reward related to the poster information.
4. Students create a visual for the poster.
5. Posters with visual, descriptive clues and clever rewards are posted in the classroom, and students share information for a cooperative learning experience.
6. Students walk around the class in pairs or groups sharing poster information and learning from each other.

Variation

- Students can leave off the names of their wanted figures from the poster, allowing peers to use descriptive poster information to identify who the figure is or what the concept is.

Sample Applications

English
- ○ Characters in a book, prominent authors

Social Studies
- Historical figures, political parties

Science
- Scientists, concepts such as elements, or energy sources

Math
- Mathematicians or concepts, such as Pythagorean theorem

World Language
- Descriptions of classmates, teachers, or other school personnel using world languages

Implementation Considerations

- Posters may be created by individual students, pairs, or small groups.
- You may provide a variety of suggested resources or a number of resources required to complete the poster; for example, students may be required to use five references listed in MLA form on the back of the poster.
- You can ask students to move posters around, creating a story.
- You can ask questions about the central concept and have students guess answers from poster information independently or in small groups.

How This Strategy Can Support Individuals With Learning Differences

- Constructing and reviewing work from the posters provides rehearsal to support learners with memory needs.
- Students with auditory needs are supported with visual learning materials.
- This can be an individual or cooperative experience to support social preferences.
- Poster information supports students with low experiential bases because it provides an opportunity to share new information and experiences.
- This strategy provides opportunities for language learners to use props and speak extemporaneously with visual cues to support language and comprehension.

Vignette Sample: Social Studies and World History

The World History class was beginning a unit on India. Mrs. G. provided each student with a Wanted Poster topic. Topics included Akbar, Mughal, Emperor, Queen Elizabeth I, Indian National Congress, Muslim League, Mohandas Gandhi, dalits, Indira Gandhi, and Panchayat (a small government in India). Students worked in pairs creating wanted posters. Students were asked to write four to five descriptors on the posters and to have at least one visual and a clever reward, leaving a blank line where the name of the figure would be. They were only given two days to complete the project. On Monday, they worked on it in class, and on Wednesday, they were asked to present. In class, students used their texts to explore a new chapter, and they were allowed to complete the rest of the assignment using at least three other references. When the posters were due, Mrs. G. asked that students present them to the full class. Students could share predictions. As a class, they studied the new unit throughout the next two weeks, and they intermittently made connections to the wanted posters displayed around the class. At these times, students who created the posters could evaluate if their peers accurately identified the topics.

For example, at the beginning of the poster session, students went around the room sharing posters. Most students knew who Mohandas Gandhi was, but no one knew who the dalits were. As the unit progressed, students shared information from posters related to their names or topics. At the end of the unit, Mrs. G. put a number on each poster and asked students to walk around in pairs identifying Wanted Poster names or topics with the right number. Most teams did very well. After the unit test, many students shared that they could remember information from posters by visualizing pictures and recalling discussion.

WANTED: FROM WIKIPEDIA

____?

- Light-brown, peaceful man with glasses seeking independence for India
- Married at 13 years old in an arranged Hindu marriage
- Born in Bombay and studied in London, becoming a barrister
- Spent many years peacefully advocating for civil rights in India
- May answer to Indian nicknames, Mahatma "Great Soul" or Bapu "Father"
- Spent time in jail for civil disobedience
- Last seen speaking to peasants about women's rights and doing away with the caste system

Reward: Independence for India

WANTED: ____?

- Once referred to as the "untouchables" in the Hindu caste system, they are considered lower than the lowest caste, the outcaste.
- Most people in this group have extreme poverty and, for very little money, clean streets and sewers.
- They have been made to parade naked and eat feces, even though caste systems were outlawed in 1950 in India.
- A few of these individuals have risen up and been voted into office.
- They were last seen in the countryside cleaning streets and sewers.

Reward: All dalits move to the top of the caste system and become Brahmins.

STRATEGY 34

We Interview

Explanation

Prior to the lesson, or unit, each student interviews a person who relates to the lesson content in some way. During the lesson, students contribute relevant information based on what they learned during the interview. The essential component of this strategy is that the interviews allow the content of the lesson to be primarily driven by the students, with teacher as facilitator organizing the flow of the information and tying the parts together.

Advance Preparation

- Make up the list of interview questions, and make a copy for each student.

Directions

1. Consider what kind of people students could interview to find out information that will enhance lesson content.
2. One or two weeks in advance, give students their assignment. You are asking students to do the following:
   - Find a person who fits the criteria set out.
   - Use the preset questions to interview.
   - Take notes during the interview.
   - Come to class on the due date prepared to share what they have learned within the context of the lesson.
   - Prepare a graphic organizer of what they learned (if you choose for students to do this as well).
3. During the lesson, include student input based on what they have learned from their interviews. For instance, as you introduce each point, ask students to give examples. Students can refer to their interview notes and graphic organizers.
4. You can also set up a chart, and during the group discussion, let students fill in their charts using the information they learned from interviews.

Sample Applications (Who Students Can Interview)

Social Studies

- A Holocaust survivor (or someone who is related to a Holocaust survivor)
- Parents or family members about family background and ancestry
- Anyone who has lived through a specific era in history or through a historical event (e.g., 9/11)
- Someone who has voted for the first time

Science/Health

- Someone about what they are doing to protect the environment.
- A doctor, nurse, pharmacist, dietician, or physical trainer, or someone else in the medical field about what adolescents can do now to protect their health in the future

English

- Someone who relates to a character, setting, or theme of a novel the class is studying
- Any adult about a positive life experience, and write an essay about it
- (The information gained from any or all of the interview suggestions here can become the subject of essays as students learn about and then practice writing various types of essays, i.e., persuasive, descriptive, narrative, expository, or process.)

Math

- Any adult about how he or she uses math in his or her current profession, getting specific examples (During class, choose any questions that relate to your selected topic. Have students create a spreadsheet or do a statistical analysis using the data collected.)

Appropriate for Adaptation to a Variety of Subjects

- Someone who is in an unusual line of work
- Someone in a position, profession, or job that students want to learn more about
- A college freshman or a high school freshman (depending on the grade level of your students)
- Any adult about taxes (what taxes they need to pay, how the process works, how it affects finances, etc.)
- Someone who has been on a job interview to find out what the process is like and how one might best prepare

Variations

- You can invite a panel to the class and conduct the interview as a group.
- Instead of handing out a list of questions, have the class work together to brainstorm the list of questions, with your input as needed. Ask students to consider what they need to know about a given topic. Remind students to keep lesson objectives in mind as they generate questions.
- For the class period in which you discuss the content, you can divide students into groups. Give each group one of the questions to discuss what they have learned, and then have each group share, summarizing what the group discussed. You can do this for any or all for the questions from the interview.
- Discuss with your students how the information from a person may or may not differ from information from other sources. Discuss other sources of information, including the media.

Implementation Considerations

- Scout out a few teachers in the school who meet the criteria for the interview, and ask if they are willing to be interviewed by your students. If a few students have difficulty finding someone on their own, you can suggest one of the teachers you have preselected.
- To make it easier for students to locate an interview person, widen the parameters of who they should be looking for. Students can also share an interview person with a classmate as needed.
- Consider using available technology to conduct interviews as needed.

How This Strategy Can Support Individuals With Learning Differences

- This strategy exposes students to multiple perspectives related to a given topic or content area. Students hear different voices, different opinions, and different experiences. The focus is not on one correct answer but on a multitude of perspectives. This is important for the student with a low experiential base, but it is equally as beneficial for all of your students.
- We Interview affords students the opportunity to practice their questioning skills as well as their listening skills. These skills not only help students to be more successful in middle and high school but also prepare them for life after high school. At the same time, students are practicing appropriate social interaction in an applied setting.
- Each student comes into the lesson with information to share. This is particularly effective for the student with auditory processing issues or communication issues, who may infrequently answer questions in class because the pace of the question-and-answer session often does not allow enough time to process the question and formulate an answer before the class is already two questions ahead. This also works for the student who may be reticent to speak out in class for any number of reasons. With We Interview, every student has relevant information to impart to the class. Structuring the lesson so that every student comes to class with something unique to share levels the playing field for that particular lesson.

Vignette Sample: Environmental Science

At the start of the school year, Mrs. L. wanted to engage her students from the beginning, help them connect to the subject matter, and answer the unasked question in the room, notably, "What is environmental science, and why are we in this classroom anyway?"

She started the year off with a discussion of what environmental science is and how it potentially affects all of our lives. Then, she challenged the class to draw up a list of all of the people they could think of that might have some relevant information about the subject matter, and after they said "scientist," they could not think of anyone else. Mrs. L. had them look through their texts, do a bit of research, and try again, and this time, she was rewarded with a substantial list of people.

(Continued)

(Continued)

The next day, she explained that each student was to find one of the people listed, or another relevant person, and interview him or her about environmental science, what it is, how its study affects the world we live in, and how as adolescents they can take what they learn into account in their everyday lives in a very practical way. After a couple (or more) groans, she started to hear a few tentative positive responses, and soon, the students were discussing who they might talk to.

The following week, students came in prepared to talk about what they learned about environmental science. The question of what environmental science is and how it affects our world and our actions was answered successfully throughout the class period by the students, based on what they learned through their interviews. Mrs. L. planned to use this strategy at least a few more times during the course of the semester and to include it in her course of study for subsequent years as well.

In addition to helping her students connect to the subject matter, and allowing the students to be the ones to drive the lesson with content, Mrs. L. saw other benefits to using this strategy over the course of the school year. We Interview provided her students with practice with real-world skills, like asking relevant questions and really listening to what other people say.

STRATEGY 35

What Would They Say?

Explanation

This strategy directs students to use their knowledge of a given topic, book, or era in history to think up phrases that famous people or fictional characters might have said. Students take turns matching up phrases with the names of those who could have said them.

Materials

- Index cards (white)
- Sentence strips (not much wider than the index cards) or index cards in light colors
- Pens or pencils

Advance Preparation

- Look at the unit you are studying, and make a list of all of the people that the students will be learning about. Write one name on each index card. You will have as many index cards as you have names of people.

Directions

1. Divide students into an even number of groups of three or four.
2. Each group gets a number of index cards with one name written on each and an equal number of blank sentence strips.
3. Model this strategy for the class using a person the class might be familiar with, either the principal of the school or the president of the United States, for example. Have the class brainstorm phrases that these individuals might have said, keeping in mind the character of the individuals and the circumstances in which they might find themselves.
4. You can encourage students to reread class notes, refer to the text, or use the computer to research each name.
5. Students work in their groups to fill out one sentence strip for each name that they have. Then, they line up the index cards on a desk and put the sentence strips in a separate pile to the side.
6. When everyone is finished, they exchange index cards and sentence strips. (An easy way to do this is to have each group leave their cards and strips on their tables, and then everyone moves to the table to the right.) The goal is for each group to read the sentence strips that their peers wrote and place them in front of the names of the people who might have said them.

7. When all the sentence strips are matched with the corresponding names, the groups can work together to check answers. Sometimes, more than one answer might make sense, and students will need to discuss their reasons for choosing a given response.
8. The teacher walks around to each group as they are working.

Sample Applications

English
- Any of the characters from a novel the class has read
- The names of several authors, poets, or playwrights
- Greek gods and goddesses

Social Studies
- Famous generals
- Famous presidents throughout the ages
- Presidential candidates
- Current events (names that are in the news)

Science
- Famous inventors
- Scientists throughout the ages (particularly appropriate for end-of-the-semester review, using names of the scientists studied)

Variations

- You can provide blank index cards, and the students can think up a list of the names they want to use.
- You can use this strategy through Number 4 and omit the part where they switch groups and guess who said what from the other groups. Instead, the strategy can end by one of the following:
  - Each student chooses one or more of the phrases they wrote and writes a paragraph or two about why this individual might have uttered this phrase, using supporting detail from class content.
  - Each student can write in his or her journal about what conclusions about the topic they were able to draw based on the work they just did.
  - This strategy can serve as a jumping-off point to an essay each student has to write.
  - When all of the groups are finished, you can give each one the opportunity to read the list of names they had to work with, along with one of their phrases, and let the rest of the class guess who said it.

Implementation Considerations

- Give one group, or all of the groups, the option to eliminate one or two of the name cards from their stacks.
- If necessary, review content as a class before you begin the strategy.

- Use additional examples to model the strategy before the students begin. You can have students think up sentences or have a sample pile already made up and invite individuals to match up the phrases with the name cards, so the class can visualize exactly what they are supposed to do.

How This Strategy Can Support Individuals With Learning Differences

- This strategy includes multiple opportunities for repetition and rehearsal as students discuss each name and what he or she might have said.
- You may want to ask groups to write lists of facts about each person for purposes of preteaching or reteaching. You can check the fact sheet if necessary or help each group to get started. The group then checks the lists they made to help them come up with ideas of what each person might have said. This adds additional structure to the task.
- The question here—"What Would They Say?"—is open-ended. This strategy encourages answers that range from concrete to the more abstract, higher-level thinking, which benefits a variety of learners. Students can compose sentences that are factual, based on concrete information (e.g., Where is my horse?), or they can create sentences based on inference and higher-order thinking.
- What Would They Say? supports metacognition. Students have to develop and use thinking strategies to figure out what phrases would be most appropriate for each person and then to match up sentence strips their peers wrote with the correct names of who might have said them.

Vignette Sample: Science—Types of Scientists

Mrs. S. decided to use this strategy halfway through the year. As she reviewed her course curriculum, she made a list of all of the different types of scientists they had discussed already and added the names of a few that they had not yet covered to test for prior knowledge.

She divided the class into six groups and gave each group a packet of index cards that included the names of seven different types of scientists, one per index card. Group 1 had the following names listed on their index cards:

Seismologist
Geologist
Cytologist
Paleontologist
Meteorologist
Ethnologist
Agronomist

(Continued)

(Continued)

They were allowed to eliminate one of the cards. The groups decided to tackle the names one at a time and use the elimination option if they came across one that they had difficulty with.

Jenna took out her textbook and offered to look up words as needed, and Samson took out his class notes for the same purpose. Roles were not assigned for this particular strategy, but Abdul turned into the natural leader. He suggested starting with a familiar term and chose the word meteorologist. *He led a group discussion about what a meteorologist does, and they discussed what this type of scientist might say. They settled on this phrase: "The jet stream location indicates that this is going to be a very cold and snowy winter for much of the country." Brian took one of the light blue index cards, wrote down the phrase, and put it aside.*

The group continued to work, asking both Jenna and Samson to look up information on the ethnologist and the agronomist. The class had not yet discussed the latter, and Brian wanted to put that one aside, but the others were curious and wanted to look up the term and see if they could figure it out in their own. They learned that the agronomist specializes in soil and crops and had a discussion about what that actually meant. The group decided to use the term after all. As Abdul said, "We can make it challenging for the group who has to match up our name cards with the phrases." (His group liked that idea!)

When the groups were finished, Mrs. S. asked each group to rotate to the right and match up the phrases with the types of scientists who might have said them. In preparation, each group made a pile of their phrase cards and laid out the scientist cards in a horizontal row.

The groups matched up the phrases with the scientists with much discussion and debate and several checks with the textbook. When all groups were finished, they moved to the right one more time to check the work the previous group did and to make changes as and if needed. Then, the group went back to check their own table to see if the words and phrases were matched up correctly. Mrs. S. closed by asking each group what they had learned.

As Abdul was leaving the classroom, he added, "That was a lot of fun, but we really had to think hard."

The Phrases That Group 1 Came Up With

Seismologist—The magnitude and the intensity of the shaking of the latest earthquake in California was far greater than for previous earthquakes.

Geologist—Are those igneous rocks?

Cytologist—Information from the cells of a person with a particular disease can give us vital information for treatment of that disease.

Paleontologist—We had a very encouraging dig at Black Water Draw.

Meteorologist—The jet stream location indicates that this is going to be very cold and snowy winter for much of the country.

Agronomist—We are learning how to grow crops that will have more nutrient value.

Group 2 matched them up correctly but really struggled with paleontologist *and* cytologist. *They had much discussion and checked their textbooks, class notes, and the Internet before making the final decision. Student answers indicated that the class had an understanding of what each of these people did.*

STRATEGY 36

The Whip

Explanation

This is a simple strategy that affords every class member the opportunity to speak. You pose a question and then whip around the room, giving each student in order a chance to respond if he or she so chooses.

Directions

1. Pose one question, or ask students to give an example related to the content that has just been covered. Choose an open-ended question that everyone can answer in their own way.
2. Ask students to respond in three sentences or less. This is an important part of the process to keep the discussion moving and to keep any one person from monopolizing a discussion.
3. One student can volunteer to go first, or you can choose the person who starts. After the first person speaks, the person to his or her right goes next. Each person in order takes his or her turn. All students know when it will be his or her turn.
4. Everyone has the option to say "pass" if he or she so chooses.
5. You can engineer who speaks first, in the middle, or closer to the end by strategically choosing where in the circle to start.

Sample Applications

Any Subject

- What character or historical figure that we have studied can you best relate to, and why?
- What did you find most interesting or surprising from today's lesson?
- Give an example of _____________.
- Which approach or formula that we learned will you use, and how (or why)?
- Name a cause and consequence of conflict.
- What is your "a-ha" moment from today's lesson?

Implementation Considerations

Timing

- This works well as closure at the end of a class period and can be adapted easily to a limited time period.
- This can be used frequently throughout the school year.

Tip

- This can be used effectively and efficiently as lesson closure for any subject or grade level.

How This Strategy Can Support Individuals With Learning Differences

- This works particularly well for individuals with auditory processing issues because they have the opportunity to hear the question, think it through, and formulate a response, and they can figure out when their turn will be so they can be prepared.
- This is also very helpful for the student who is less likely to volunteer to speak up in class, particularly the individual who
  - has difficulty taking risks with answering questions,
  - is unsure of the content,
  - is an English Language Learner,
  - has language issues or is struggling with expressive language, or
  - has a more quiet or shy personality.
- The structure of this strategy works equally well for the student who tends to dominate the conversation.
- The quick pace of this strategy supports individuals who easily lose focus.

Vignette Sample

Mr. Y. uses the Whip in all of his classes, from ninth grade through twelfth grade. As a result, he feels that his classes have easy flows of discussion and dialogue, and his students generally listen to their peers.

What he found most interesting was the response of his students. Frequently, in the last 10 or so minutes, he would pose an open-ended question based on the content and whip around quickly, giving each student "air time" to reflect on learning that took place that day. This is generally an integral part of class time. Over the past two years, he has noticed that his students, particularly those from grades 10 through 12, have started to incorporate the same strategy in their class group presentations.

STRATEGY 37

Why and Because

Explanation

Students use graphic organizers during a content-intensive lesson to make meaningful connections between key points. The *why* refers to the key points that happened, and the *because* refers to the surrounding causes, effects, or details that explain them in more depth.

Materials

- Copies of the template, one for each student

Advance Preparation

- Prepare the Why and Because template—in each of the small, inverted triangles, fill in one of the major points that you want students to understand from the day's lesson. (You should have approximately between four and seven top triangles filled in.) Leave the bottom triangle in each pair blank.

Directions

1. Explain the graphic organizer worksheet that will serve as the framework for this lesson. This will focus students in on what to be listening for.
2. Remind students that, throughout the lesson, you will be elaborating on each of the key points written in the small, inverted triangles.
3. Instruct students to take notes during the lesson. When you have finished, let students work in groups to complete their worksheets. Remind them that the lesson for the day was organized around the key points listed in each triangle and that they are to now answer the *because* triangle to explain the corresponding point in greater depth.
4. Alternately, you can pause and let students gather their thoughts and fill in the large triangles one or more times during the course of the lesson, as needed, or you can incorporate this structure into the lesson and discuss and fill them out as a whole class as you go along.

Variations

- The terms *Why* and *Because* can be changed to the following:
  - cause and effect
  - fact and details
  - category and examples
  - whatever else fits a particular lesson

Sample Applications

Science

- Space exploration
- Climate change
- Sustainable ecosystems

Math

- How to use matrices to represent data

English

- Writing a persuasive essay
- How to write a research paper
- Symbolism and irony in any given novel (*Animal Farm* is but one example of a relevant novel)
- The study of human behavior (can fit into English, Psychology, and Social studies)
- Maslow's hierarchy on needs and how this affects human behavior

Implementation Considerations

- This strategy can be implemented with the whole class as the structure of the lesson, or students can complete the template individually, or they can work in small groups.
- The graphic organizer can be varied according to the difficulty of the subject and the grade and ability level of the class. The *why* triangles can be left blank as well, and students can be held responsible to fill in both the *why* and the *because* in each set. Use this option to provide more of a challenge.

How This Strategy Can Support Individuals With Learning Differences

- This strategy provides a concrete structure to help students organize a large body of knowledge in a meaningful way.
- The completed graphic organizer becomes an effective study guide and highlights for students what information is most important.
- The intention is that this is a skill that students can generalize and use in other subject areas as needed, as well (in this case, teaching students how to learn as well as teaching them subject matter).
- This strategy supports students who have difficulties with retention using only auditory memory and auditory processing.

Vignette Sample: Health

Mrs. B.'s class was taking part in D.A.R.E., the Drug Abuse Resistance Education program that gives kids the skills they need to avoid involvement in drugs, gangs, and violence. D.A.R.E. is a police officer–led series of classroom lessons for students from kindergarten through 12th grade, and it is now in 75% of our nation's school districts. Mrs. B. was pleased that her district was able to take part in this important program.

She planned a unit on inhalants as a follow-up unit to reinforce and expand on the lessons from the D.A.R.E. officer. Because there was such a wealth of material and the topic was such a current one, she wanted to help her students to stay focused and be able to organize the material in a meaningful way. She decided to use the Why and Because strategy.

In preparation, Mrs. B. identified seven key points for this particular lesson—the information that she wanted her students to focus on. She then used the strategy template and filled in the top, small inverted triangle for each of the seven triangle pairs, putting one key idea in each. She left the larger, bottom right-side-up triangle blank for her students to fill out.

She needed her students to understand that, even though inhalants may seem harmless, they can actually be quite dangerous.

Each of the key points in the lesson was written into one of the smaller, inverted top triangles as the WHY:

Triangle pair #1
The WHY: Inhalants can seem harmless, but they can be very dangerous.
The BECAUSE (filled in by the students):

(Mrs. B. was looking for student answers about the dangerous effects of the chemicals in inhalants and how teenagers can overlook these dangers because they are used in everyday supplies.)

Triangle pair #2
The WHY: Why are inhalants so dangerous?
The BECAUSE (filled in by the students):

(Mrs. B. was looking for student answers about how teenagers think there's no harm in using inhalants only a few times and how easy they are to find—even at home.)

Triangle pair #3
The WHY: Why are inhalants able to affect people so quickly?
The BECAUSE (filled in by the students):

(Mrs. B. was looking for "when chemicals are inhaled, the lungs absorb these chemicals into the bloodstream very quickly, sending them throughout the brain and body.")

Triangle pair #4
The WHY: Why are inhalants so easy for teenagers to find?
The BECAUSE (filled in by the students):

Triangle pair #5
The WHY: What happens when these common household items are inhaled that makes them so dangerous?
The BECAUSE (filled in by the students):

Mrs. B. explained the strategy to her students and started her lesson. She paused for a few minutes every so often to let them get caught up with their worksheets. She felt that, by filling in the small triangles for her class, it gave them signals or guideposts—things to listen for during the lesson. She did notice that, each time she emphasized one of the key points, students became a bit more attentive. (She noticed this through body language, eye contact, rustling of papers, and picking up of pencils.) Why and Because helped her students to discern a tangible structure within the lesson, and this helped them to follow along.

Template for Why and Because

Name ______________________ **Date** ______________________

Lesson Topic ____

1. why

because

2. why

because

3. why

because

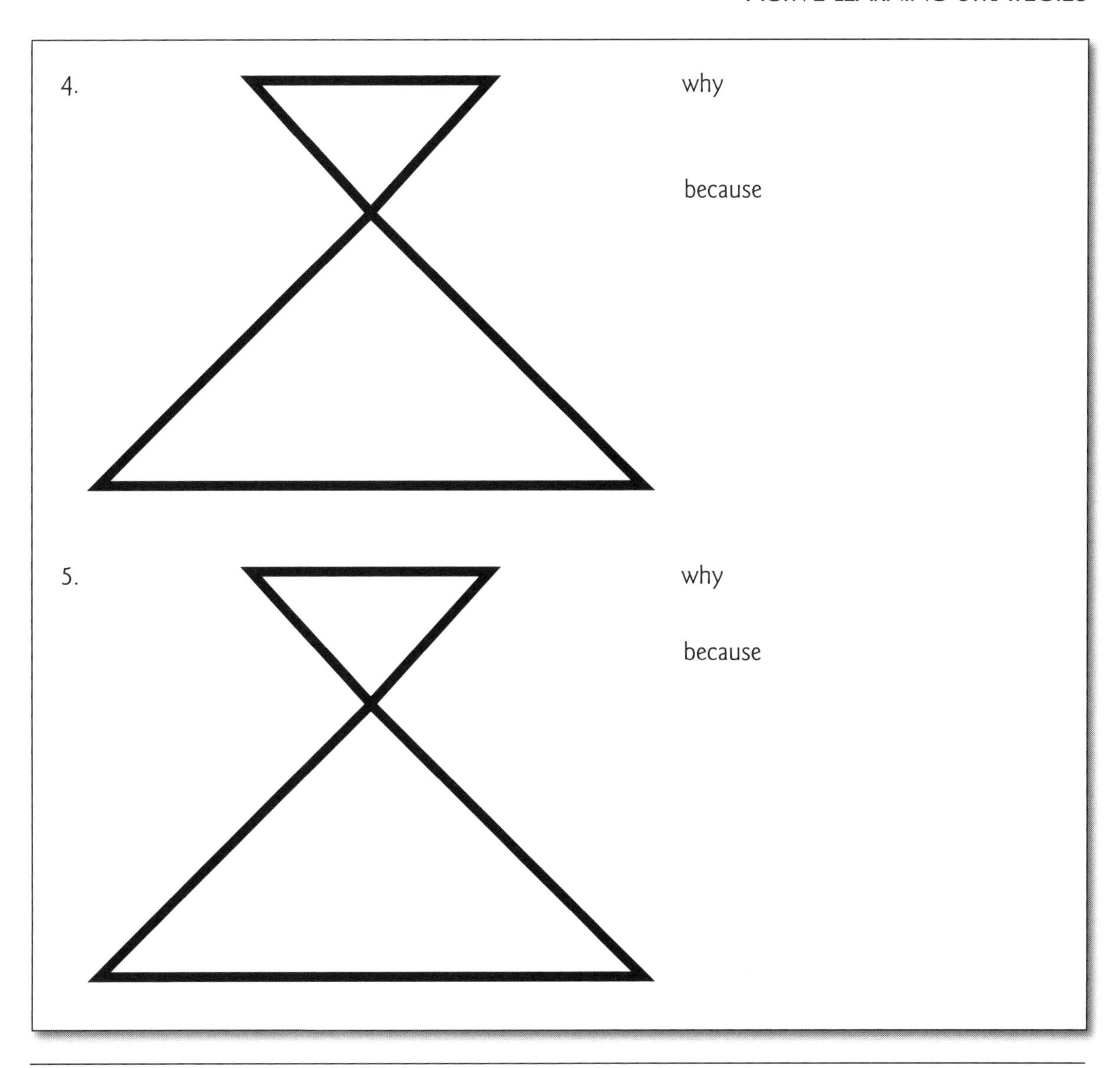
4.
why
because
5.
why
because

STRATEGY 38

Word by Word

Explanation

Buildings are built one brick at a time, and great novels are written one word at a time. This strategy challenges students to review their notes and to sum up a topic in one single word, the word that they feel symbolizes the essence of the story, the topic, or the material covered. They include explanations as to why this particular word was chosen. This works because it encourages students to think about the material, to synthesize what they have learned, and to make their own connections to the content. It is like going one step further than asking them to put something into their own words.

Advance Preparation

- Practice this strategy yourself before you challenge your students to do it. It will give you an idea of the mental processes your students will be using and will provide you with an example to share with the class.

Directions

1. Teach your lesson as planned, and encourage students to take notes.
2. At a logical stopping point, tell students that you will give them some time to look over their notes and the course textbook, if relevant, to come up with one word that they feel is reflective of the content.
3. When they come up with their one word, ask them to write up a rationale to explain their choice.
4. Ask students to volunteer to share their words, and explanations, with the class.

Variations

- After the words have been chosen individually, let students choose groups, and ask each group to create a visual that incorporates each of the words the group members used. They can have colored pencils and poster board or create their visuals using technology. Creativity is encouraged.
- During the discussion portion of the lesson, list each of the words that students have chosen and display in the classroom; let students keep this list as a study sheet.

Sample Applications

English
- ○ A short story or a poem

- ○ A novel, chapter by chapter—have each student choose one word that captures the essence of each chapter, one chapter at a time (At the end of the book, they will have gathered notes that can help them to identify important themes. See template.)
- ○ A character in a novel—students each choose a character who is intriguing to them; for each chapter that they read, they write down one word that best describes that character and his or her actions, thoughts, or feelings in that particular chapter (When the book is finished, let students celebrate each of the characters in the book. See template.)
- ○ A play

Social Studies

- ○ Propaganda (students may choose words like self-serving, misleading, untruth, nefarious)
- ○ The Olympic Games
- ○ Protest songs
- ○ Terrorism

Science

- ○ The study of pollution
- ○ Laboratory safety procedures

Implementation Considerations

- Emphasize to students that there are no right or wrong answers here. What is important is that they are able to explain why they chose particular words.
- Distilling the essence of material into one word encourages higher-order thinking and helps students to synthesize a body of knowledge into what is most meaningful.
- Consider allowing students to use technology, like an online dictionary or thesaurus.
- Consider practicing this strategy first with content the students are more familiar with, or give them a fun example before they try this with new content.

How This Strategy Can Support Individuals With Learning Differences

- Each student can work at his or her own pace.
- This open-ended strategy allows for creativity. Answers can be literal or abstract, and they can be simple, or short, or complex; all answers are correct as long as students are able to justify their responses. The needs of learners at all levels of understanding are addressed.
- The completed template can serve as a well-organized study guide.
- Consider modeling this for your students before you ask them to do it. Identify your subject matter, state what your one word is, and explain your rationale for choosing that particular word.

- To help all students to be successful (depending on grade level and student ability), introduce this strategy with a familiar concept, and have the class work together to brainstorm possible one-word descriptors. Students then choose one word from the list and write up their reasons why. The next time, use the strategy as designed.

Vignette Sample: History

Ms. D.'s class was studying space exploration and was currently learning about the Apollo space program. She talked about the space program in general and the quest to put a man on the moon in particular and explained the chronology of the Apollo missions. She decided to use the Word by Word strategy to give students the opportunity to reflect on some of the famous quotes from this era in American history.

She asked students to write down one word for each quote and then explain why they choose that particular word.

Apollo 13 was called a "successful failure" by Jim Lovell, and Ms. D. asked her class to consider what that meant. Jessica wrote down "humankind," and Nia wrote down the word "people." Both had similar explanations, focusing on the fact that it was amazing the astronauts were able to make it back to Earth safely and was more important than the fact that the actual task of the mission itself was not completed. Adam used the word "progress," explaining that, even though the crew was not able to walk on the moon, they made progress in terms of the space program itself. Shawn choose the term "knowledge," and explained that knowing what to avoid in the future gave the mission a measure of success, even though the actual mission was not completed.

Ms. D. continued the strategy with more quotes, including one more from Apollo 13—"Houston, we have a problem" from Jack Swigert—and another from Neil Armstrong from Apollo 11—"That's one small step for man, one giant leap for mankind." For each quote, she had the students fill out the template, writing down and then explaining their word choices and then adding descriptive words from their classmates. Emma and Zach each came up with particularly thoughtful responses for the Neil Armstrong quote, which led the class into an interesting discussion of man's quest to walk on the moon.

Ms. D. used this strategy with additional content during this unit. At the end of the unit, students were asked to write essays about the American space program, and Ms. D. encouraged them to refer back to their Word by Word notes.

Afterward, Ms. D. reflected on the use of the strategy. When she first began to use it, it was among much grumbling from the students. They initially found it hard to distill the essence of a body of content into one word. It did not become easy, per se, as the class became more accustomed to the process, but she noticed that it generated a lot of thought and discussion as her students were intent on each choosing just the right word.

Name Jessica

Topic Apollo 13 was called a "successful failure" by Jim Lovell

The word is: *humankind*

Because: *it was amazing that the astronauts were able to make it back to Earth safe, and it was more important than the fact that the actual task of the mission itself was not completed.*

After listening to my classmates share their words, additional words I would incorporate are:

people

knowledge

progress

victory

process

Because:

After listening to my classmates, I realized that, even if we do not reach our goals (in this case, having a person walk on the moon), we can learn so much along the way; the quote spoke to both the importance of the journey and the importance of human life. It made me think of how something can be a success even though one part of the mission did not succeed as planned.

Word-by-Word Template for a Novel

Name ____

Novel ____

Directions: For each chapter, choose ONE word that you feel is most reflective of that chapter, and explain why.

Chapter 1
The word is:

Because:

Chapter 2
The word is:

Because:

Chapter 3
The word is:

Because:

Chapter 4
The word is:

Because:

Chapter 5
The word is:

Because:

Chapter 6
The word is:

Because:

Word-by-Word Template for a Topic/Subject Matter

Name ____

Topic ____

The word is:

Because:

After listening to my classmates share their words, additional words I would incorporate are:

Because:

Word-by-Word Template to Describe a Person

(a political or historical figure, an author, a scientist, a character in a novel or a play)

The word is:

Because:

STRATEGY 39

Word Cloud

Explanation

Students brainstorm words germane to a particular topic. They use a website to input these words and create a visual that symbolizes significant themes or occurrences related to the topic.

Materials

- Computer(s) and a printer

Advance Preparation

- Make a Word Cloud on a completely different subject to use as a model for students. (You can construct your own at wordle.com or use samples from the website.)

Directions

1. Log on to the website www.wordle.net. (Directions may vary depending on the number of available computers.)
2. If this is the first time you are using this strategy, introduce it by asking the students to think of one word that comes to mind when you say the word *summer*. (Directions 2 through 6 show how to model the strategy.)
3. One at a time, let students come up to the computer and type in their word. In the case of more than one student choosing the same word, that word just gets typed in again, and again, if need be. A repeated word is an integral step in the process.
4. If you want to use two words together (i.e., large waves), type a tilde between the words (large~waves).
5. When everyone has had a chance to type in a word, follow directions on the website, hit the indicated key, and up will pop a Word Cloud or *wordle*.
6. Have your students discuss what they see (the words that are more common are larger, and the words that are less frequent are smaller.) Ask students what this means, what it says about themes, and what they learned about the topic.
7. Then, get students into groups of four or five, and pose a topic based on the lesson or unit of study. You can make as many groups as there are computers, or you can give each group a turn at the computer.
8. Give the class a few minutes for each student to write his or her own list of three to five words that seem most significantly related to the topic. You can

allow students to look at the course text, class notes, or other sources if you so choose. This section of the strategy should be done individually without conferring with classmates.

9. When individual lists are completed, students get back together in their small groups. Depending on the number of computers available, each group can work at their own computer, or each group is given a turn at the computer.
10. When each group has their turn, have them log on to http://www.wordle.net. Following the directions on the website, each person types in every word that she or he has listed. It is fine for a word to be repeated many times.
11. When all of the words have been typed in, the group follows the website's directions, hits the appropriate key, and completes the Word Cloud.
12. Have each group print the Word Cloud they have created. (One way to do this is to hit *Print Screen* and then to save the document in a PowerPoint.)
13. Give groups a few minutes to discuss what their visuals represent, what key themes emerged as a result of creating the word clouds.
14. Students reconvene as a whole class, and each group has the opportunity to show their Word Cloud to the class and discuss the implications of the visual they have created. Encourage discussion and comparison among the word clouds. If each group had a similar topic to work with, what were the similarities and differences in the finished products? What themes emerged class-wide? What does this tell us about ____________ (fill in the class topic here)?

Variations

- Possible sentence stems for which one- or two-word answers are possible include the following:
  - What do you think of when I say the word ________________?
  - What is your favorite ________________?
  - What is one recurring theme in ________________?
  - In one word, how would you describe ________________?
- Use the Word Cloud to show frequency of occurrence. Ask students to track a particular character in a play and write down many times he or she did various things. In this case, each group can focus on a different character. This can also be used to poll a group of people and use the Word Cloud to visually record and illustrate responses.
- After each group has created a Word Cloud, instead of reconvening for a whole-class discussion, ask students to return to their seats. Let one member of each group hang up his or her visual in the front of the classroom. Ask students to look over the work that each group has produced and then write in their journals (or write essays) about what this says about the topic.

- Let students look at the word clouds from each of the other groups. Each student has to choose three to five words that he or she agrees with from one of the word clouds and write an essay about why these words are significant as related to the topic.
- Have students pose questions to teachers in the school or the members of their homerooms (e.g., ask all English teachers who their favorite authors are). Remind students to ask questions that require one- or two-word answers.

Sample Applications

English
- What are the important themes in *To Kill a Mockingbird*?
- What messages from Shakespeare's plays translate into modern times?
- Use one word to describe how you felt after reading the novel, short story, or play.

Social Studies
- What themes do you feel most closely relate to the Great Depression?
- What are the results of a war?
- Which words represent the United States Constitution (sample words: constitution, president, United~States, legislature, authority, laws, power, citizen, amendments, Congress, congressmen, senators, senate)?

Science
- What scientific invention do you feel is most important?

Implementation Considerations

- If there is only one or a few computers in the classroom, and students have to share, this is a good strategy to combine with a group assignment.
- This strategy can be broken up into more than one class period, if time allows, while continuing the study of the topic. Give one class period to introduce the strategy and to have students develop their word lists, use the computer, and discuss the results among themselves and the next class period for sharing with the class and whole-class discussion. Both days, the focus can be on the topic.

How This Strategy Can Support Individuals With Learning Differences

- The very visual nature of this strategy supports visual learners and students who have issues with auditory processing.
- The finished product, which can be turned into a poster, supports memory. It can be posted in the classroom as a visual reference.
- Students can refer to the finished product to come up with talking points—this supports individuals who may struggle with language and may benefit from visual prompts.
- This strategy can take something that is subtle and make it more concrete.

Vignette Sample: Math—Decimals

Mrs. G.'s class was studying decimals. Using technology as a research tool, she wanted her students to find facts about how decimals occur in everyday life. She had students get into groups, and she asked why they thought they needed to learn about decimals. The answers were amusing, to say the least, but they were not on target.

She asked the students to research how decimal facts were actually a part of everyday life using the Internet as well as a WebQuest that she designed for the class. (A WebQuest is "an inquiry-oriented activity in which some or all of the information that learners interact with comes from resources on the Internet, optionally supplemented with videoconferences," according to Bernie Dodge, the originator of WebQuests at http://webquest.sdsu.edu/about_webquests.html). Once they realized that technology was a part of math class, they were enthusiastic to get started. As the class was involved in their research, their lists of words grew longer. Mrs. G. heard, "Wow, I didn't know that real people actually use decimals," and, "Decimals—money—shopping, cool."

Each group, amidst much discussion about decimals, came up with a long list of real-life examples, typed these carefully into the computer, pushed the correct keys, and a wordle appeared. See an example of the list, and wordle, from Group I below.

Group I was interested in the finished product and continued their discussion about what they had learned. Referring to the completed wordle, Lewis pointed out that professional baseball players use decimals all the time, and Keely added that we see decimals all the time just reading a menu or shopping. The group was really interested in comparing which words were little, and which ones were larger, and what that meant in terms of how often the words were chosen.

Mrs. G. asked the class to reconvene and to share what they had learned, and as closure, she had each student write in his or her math journal about how decimals are used in everyday life and how the understanding of decimals will affect them as adults.

As her students wrote, Mrs. G. reflected on the lesson. It was true that the class had an increased appreciation of decimals and the role of math in real life, to be sure, but she was most pleased about the student involvement. Even her more reluctant learners were taking active parts in the research and in the small group discussions, and she was looking forward to reading the math journals that evening. As students left for their next classes, Mrs. G. hung up the word clouds on the back bulletin board.

Source: The vignette is based on a lesson by Kelly Gallo, Centenary College education student.

An Example of a Word Cloud on the Topic of Decimals

STRATEGY 40

Zip-It (Also Known as Baggie Stories)

Explanation

After reading an assignment or learning new content, students work in small groups to write up and illustrate a portion of what they have read (or learned) on a plastic baggie. Each group presents their work, in sequential order, if appropriate, and as they present, they create a visual as each baggie panel is zipped to the previous one and displayed on the overhead. The competed visual tells the story and can be displayed in the classroom if desired.

Materials

- Ziploc plastic bags, sandwich size or quart sized (have enough for one for each group plus have extras on hand as needed)
- Permanent, fine-tipped magic markers in a variety of colors (must be permanent markers)
- One pair of scissors

Advance Preparation

- The directions for how to make and use baggie stories come from *Differentiated Instructional Strategies for Reading in the Content Areas* by Carolyn Chapman and Rita King, Corwin Press, 2003. We have adopted their idea and elaborated on it.
- In order to prepare the plastic bags, follow these steps:
  1. Use one Ziploc plastic bag for each cooperative group in the classroom.
  2. Cut each bag down both sides and open it out flat. Hold it vertically, with the shortest side at the top.
  3. Students may want to zip the bags together to see which side the writing will show up on when they are zipped together when the project is completed. Have them place marks at the tops of the flattened bags on the sides that the students will need to write on.
  4. Separate the baggies for students to use.
  5. Try this out on your own before you do it in class, so you are familiar with the technicalities of how it all fits together.

Directions

1. Pass out one bag per cooperative group, and be sure to show each group exactly where to position the flattened baggie as they get ready to write on it. This is important because the baggies will be zipped together, and you will need the writing to be in the same direction for all of the baggies, so it can be read easily.

2. "Each group is assigned one element, attribute, fact, detail, step or passage of the assignment" (Chapman & King, p. 81). Each group is assigned a different part of the content to focus on.
3. Give students time to read the assignment, or take part in direct instruction.
4. When students have finished reading, each group is directed to draw on the top part of the bag and write a caption on the bottom part.
5. Each group discusses what is most important in their section of the material and how they should illustrate it. They draw on the top half of their flattened baggie and write an explanation below it.
6. Decide on the order that groups will present to the class. This will be more of an issue if the content is sequential.
7. Gather the bags, and zip them together in sequential order so that the continuous line of baggie pictures tells a story in logical order.
8. Each group goes to the overhead and presents their part on their bag as it rolls across the overhead. This gives students a very concrete sense of how all of the material fits together.
9. When the lesson is over, tape colored construction paper behind the long plastic baggie column, and hang it up in the classroom. This will serve as a visual reinforcer of lesson content.

Sample Applications

Social Studies

- The study of a timeline
- The events that led to the rise and the fall of Communism
- The history of political parties in the United States
- The roles assigned to individuals in a caste system

Science

- Elements of the periodic table
- The steps in the scientific method

English

- "Beowulf," or another poem in Old English—each group summarizes the meaning of one stanza (bottom half of baggie) and provides an illustration to go with it (top half of baggie)
- The acts of a play that the class has been studying (one for each group)

Math

- Advanced word problems

World Language

- The sequence of a given task (e.g., making a sandwich, starting with buying the ingredients) using the language they are studying

Implementation Considerations

Construction

- This is simple once you have put the bags together so that the writing and pictures will all be facing the same direction when the baggies are zipped together.

How This Strategy Can Support Individuals With Learning Differences

This is effective in the inclusion classroom for a variety of reasons:

- The novelty of the baggie and the materials used can work to increase both interest in and attention to the task at hand.
- It appeals to visual, kinesthetic, and tactile learners.
- It accommodates a variety of strengths.
- When each group processes out, the content of the lesson is broken down into clear, sequential steps, compete with illustrations. There is ample reinforcement of content.
- As each baggie is attached to the previous one, there is an oral explanation. This is coupled with the visual representation of literally zipping part one to part two to part three—a very concrete way of illustrating the connection between the events. This has the benefit of pairing both auditory and visual stimuli and connecting parts to the whole.

Related Information and Resources

Chapman and King (2003) have developed 12 examples of response books that teachers can use to differentiate instruction in the classroom. The authors explain that response books can be used "for content assignments for reviews using different formats of book design and shapes, textures of paper, writing fonts, and implements" (p. 79).

We feel that response books support a variety of learners, allowing for rehearsal and reinforcement of content. We have borrowed one of their examples, baggie stories, and have used it as a strategy. Interestingly, we have found this strategy particularly well suited to the themes and content studied in middle and high school, and it has been received enthusiastically by said students.

Vignette Sample: Literature

Mrs. F.'s class had just finished reading "Death of a Salesman." She divided the class in half arbitrarily and asked each section to subdivide themselves into four groups. She gave each section the materials, as noted above, and then explained what they needed to do.

Each section of the class was to be responsible for producing one complete Zip-it baggie story of the play, a visual with both words and illustrations on plastic bags.

(Continued)

(Continued)

Each group had the following instructions:

Group I was responsible for the first half of Act I.

Group 2 was responsible for the second half of Act I.

Group 3 was responsible for the first half of Act II.

Group 4 was responsible for the second half of Act II.

Each group was encouraged to review their class notes, the text of the play, and any supporting web material. They were asked to illustrate the top halves of their baggies with pictures evocative of their portions of the play and to add written descriptions on the bottom halves of the same baggies. When baggies were complete, Group I attached their baggie to that of Group 2, who zipped it to that of Group 3, and so on. The result was two complete descriptions of Death of a Salesman *on baggies, one from each section of the class.*

The first section put their baggies on an overhead and took turns reading their descriptions and showing their illustrations for Act I and then Act II. This was followed by the presentation from the second section. Mrs. F. asked the students to note similarities and differences in each summary and to discuss what they learned about the play.

As Mrs. F. left class at the end of the period, she was surprised how effective this was in getting her students to think. The discussion was insightful, and students appeared to be engaged throughout the lesson. She packed up for the day as she thought about how else she might incorporate this strategy.

Source: Adapted from Chapman & King (2003).

STRATEGY 41

Closure

Explanation

Closure is typically used at the end of a lesson to reinforce key concepts, help organize student thinking, and help students relate new content to prior knowledge. Closure is student centered. This is the opportunity for the students, not the teacher, to talk. Closure is an important part of any lesson, but it can also qualify as an active learning strategy.

While important, Closure is often overlooked or skipped over because of time constraints. We have taught many lessons where we are rushing to finish all of the material before the bell rings, and Closure was one more thing to "add on" in our effort to beat the clock.

Nevertheless, Closure facilitates learning and retention. All learners benefit from closure because it gives them the opportunity to reflect on, summarize, and focus on key points. Closure provides the opportunity for review and for students to make their own connections to what they have learned. This is a key factor for all learners and imperative for learners who have issues with processing, attention, or memory.

Some Quick Closure Ideas for When Time Is Running Very Tight

- Tell students to turn to a partner and tell her or him the most important thing they learned today.
- Ask students to write three new facts in their journals.
- Explain that one person from each row, or each section of the room, can answer the Closure question (students self-select).
- Tell the students that everyone who is wearing sneakers (or jeans, or something green, or has blond hair or who was born in January, whatever works best) will be answering the Closure question (you can differentiate seamlessly here because you have some control over who is or is not asked to answer, and you can control for time by identifying something that includes many speakers, or just a few, or by limiting the response to one sentence or less, depending on the prompt you give).

Possible Closure Questions

- What was your ah-ha moment from today's lesson?
- Was there anything we covered that surprised you?
- Tell one important point that you learned.
- Give one example of how you can use or apply what we learned to real life.
- We talked about _____ today—give us a specific example.
- Connect something we learned today to something you already knew or something we have studied previously.

A number of the strategies in this book also work well as Closure and can be used with one of the questions above. Some strategies can be used to provide Closure quickly (e.g., the Whip and Exit Cards), while others are more appropriate for when you have additional time at the end of a lesson or to wrap up a unit of study.

The following strategies lend themselves particularly well to Closure:

Name of Strategy	*Quick*	*Longer*	*Time Adjusts as Needed*	*Preparation*
Ball Toss	X		X	Prepare ball ahead of time
Exit Cards	X			Have index cards available (or have students use notebook paper)
Listening Teams		X	X	Set up teams at the beginning of the lesson and have cards ready for them; teams share at the end of the lesson as Closure
Next	X			No preparation—can be used as a review of prior knowledge or a reading at the beginning of the period, or as lesson review and reinforcement at the end of a lesson
Puzzle Pieces	X			Cards have to be prepared in advance
Spiderweb	X	X	X	Have a ball of yarn and scissors at the ready
The Whip	X			No preparation
Word by Word	X		X	No preparation
Word Cloud	X	X	X	Have a computer and the wordle website available; students type in words that relate to the lesson you have just taught and create a wordle as Closure

In addition, for some of our strategies, like Why and Because and Theme Boards, students create visuals that embody or synthesize lesson content. Having students review or reflect on this work can provide effective Closure for those lessons.

And, for Closure for this chapter, which strategy sounds particularly interesting to you, and why?

____

____

____

____

____

____

____

____

References

Anderman, E. M., & Maehr, M. L. (1994). Motivation and schooling in the middle grades. *Review of Educational Research, 64*, 287–309.

Aronson, E. (2000–2012). Jigsaw in 10 easy steps. *Jigsaw Classroom* (website). Social Psychology Network. Retrieved from http://www.jigsaw.org/steps.htm

Barthelemy-Ruiz, C., Carpier, B., & Argine, N.C. (1995). *Passages*. The United Nations High Commissioner for Refugees.

Bender, W. (2002). *Differentiating instruction for students with learning disabilities: Best practices for general and special educators.* Thousand Oaks, CA: Corwin.

Bender, W. (2008). *Differentiating instruction for students with learning disabilities: Best teaching practices for general and special educators.* Thousand Oaks, CA: Corwin Press and Council for Exceptional Children.

Benson, B. P. (2009). *How to meet standards, motivate students, and still enjoy teaching! Four practices that improve student learning.* Thousand Oaks, CA: Corwin.

Bonwell, C. C., & Eisen, J. A. (1991). Active learning: Creating excitement in the classroom. (ASHE-ERIC Higher Education Report No. 1). Washington, DC: George Washington University, School of Education and Human Development.

Brophy, J. E. (1997). *Motivating students to learn.* New York: McGraw Hill.

Bruneau-Balderrama, O. (1997). Inclusion: Making it work for teachers, too. *Clearing House, 70*(6), 328–330.

Carroll, L., & Leander, S. (2001, January). Improving student motivation through the use of active learning strategies (Master of the Arts Action Research Project). (ERIC Document Reproduction Service No. ED455961)

Chapman, C., & King, R. (2003). *Differentiated instructional strategies for reading in the content areas.* Thousand Oaks, CA: Corwin.

Checkley, K. (2005, April). The adolescent learner. *Educational Leadership, 62*(7), 96.

Choate, J. S. (2004). Basic principles and practices of inclusive instruction. In J. S. Choate (Ed.), *Successful inclusive teaching: Proven ways to detect and correct special needs* (pp. 2–17). Boston: Pearson.

Cook, B. G. (2002). Inclusive attitudes, strengths, and weaknesses of pre-service general educators enrolled in a curriculum infusion teacher preparation program. *Teacher Education and Special Education, 25*(3), 262–277.

Corney, G., & Reid, A. (2007). Student teachers' learning about subject matter and pedagogy in education for sustainable development. *Environmental Education Research, 13*(1), 33–54.

Dewey, J. (1926). *Democracy and education.* New York: Macmillan.

Dieker, L. (2007). *Demystifying secondary inclusion: Powerful school-wide and classroom strategies.* Port Chester, NY: Dude.

Duez, D. (2009). *Using philosophical chairs.* Retrieved from http://www.scribd.com/mrduez/d/12410807-Using-Philosophical-Chairs

Fenwick, T. J. (2001). *Experiential learning: A theoretical critique from five perspectives.* Columbus, OH: ERIC Clearinghouse.

Friend, M. (2010). *Interactions: Collaboration skills for school professionals.* Boston: Pearson.

Friend, M., & Bursuck, W. D. (2002). *Including students with special needs: A practical guide for classroom teachers.* Boston: Pearson.

Friend, M., & Bursuck, W. D. (2009). *Including students with special needs: A practical guide for classroom teachers.* Upper Saddle River, NJ: Merrill/Prentice Hall.

Gable, R. A., & Hendrickson, J. M. (2004). Teaching all students: A mandate for educators. In J. S. Choate (Ed.), *Successful inclusive teaching: Proven ways to detect and correct special needs* (pp. 2–17). Boston: Pearson.

Ginsberg, M. B. (2005, July). Cultural diversity, motivation, and differentiation. *Theory Into Practice, 44*(3), 218–255.

Gore, M. C. (2010). *Inclusion strategies for secondary classrooms: Keys for struggling learners.* Thousand Oaks, CA: Corwin.

Green, L. S., & Casale-Giannola, D. (2011). *40 active learning strategies for the inclusive classroom, grades K–5.* Thousand Oaks, CA: Corwin.

Gregory, G. H., & Kuzmich, L. (2004). *Data-driven differentiation in the standards-based classroom.* Thousand Oaks, CA: Corwin.

Guillaume, A. M., Yopp, R. H., & Yopp, H. K. (2007). *Strategies for active teaching: Engaging K–12 learners in the classroom.* Upper Saddle River, NJ: Pearson.

Hallahan, D. P., & Kauffman, J. M. (2006). *Exceptional learners: Introduction to special education.* Upper Saddle River, NJ: Pearson.

Hallahan, D. P., & Kauffman, J. M. (2010). *Exceptional learners: Introduction to special education.* Upper Saddle River, NJ: Pearson.

Hallahan, D. P., Kauffman, J. M., & Pullen, P. C. (2010). *Exceptional learners: An introduction to special education* (10th ed.). Upper Saddle River, NJ: Pearson.

Heacox, D. (2002). *Differentiating instruction in the regular classroom: How to reach and teach all learners, Grades 3–12.* Minneapolis, MN: Free Spirit.

Hollas, B. (2007). *Differentiating instruction in a whole-group setting: Taking the easy first steps into differentiation.* Peterborough, NH: Crystal Springs Books.

Jarolimek, J., & Foster, C. (1981). *Teaching and learning in the elementary school* (2nd ed.). New York: MacMillan.

Jensen, E. (2000). Moving with the brain in mind. *Educational Leadership, 58*(3), 34–37.

Jensen, E. (2001). *Arts with the brain in mind.* Alexandria, VA: Association for Supervision and Curriculum Development.

Jones, R. C. (2006). Carousel brainstorm. *Strategies for Reading Comprehension.* Winston-Salem, NC: Reading Quest. Retrieved from http://www.readingquest.org/strat/carousel.html

Kame'enui, E. J., Carnine, D. W., Dixon, R. C., Simmons, D. C., & Coyne, M. D. (2002). *Effective teaching strategies that accommodate diverse learners.* Upper Saddle River, NJ: Pearson.

Karten, T. J. (2005). *Inclusion strategies that work! Research-based methods for the classroom.* Thousand Oaks, CA: Corwin.

Karten, T. (2009). *Inclusion strategies that work for adolescent learners!* Thousand Oaks, CA: Corwin.

King-Shaver, B., & Hunter, A. (2003). *Differentiating instruction in the English classroom: Content, product and assessment.* Portsmouth, NH: Heinemann.

Kounin, J. S. (1977). *Discipline and group management in classrooms.* Huntington, NH: Krieger.

Lent, R. C. (2006). *Engaging adolescent learners: A guide for content area for teachers.* Portsmouth, NH: Heinemann.

Lenz, B. K., & Deshler, D. (2004). *Teaching content to all: Evidence-based inclusive practices in middle and secondary schools.* Boston: Pearson.

Lewis, L. B., & Doorlag, D. H. (2006). *Teaching special students in general education classrooms.* Upper Saddle River, NJ: Pearson.

Maday, T. (2008). Stuck in the middle: Strategies to engage middle level learners. *LD Online.* Retrieved February 27, 2011, from http://www.ldonline.org/article/Stuck_in_the_Middle:_Strategies_to_Engage_Middle-Level_Learners?theme=print

Mastropieri, M. (2001). Is the glass half full or half empty? Challenges encountered by first-year special education teachers. *Journal of Special Education, 35*(2), 66–75.

Mastropieri, M., & Scruggs, T. (2000). *The inclusive classroom: Strategies for effective instruction.* Upper Saddle River, NJ: Merrill/Prentice Hall.

Merriam-Webster Online. (2010). Retrieved February 27, 2011, from http://www.merriam-webster.com

Muraski, W. W. (2009). *Collaborative teaching in secondary schools: Making the co-teaching marriage work!* Thousand Oaks, CA: Corwin.

National Dissemination Center for Children with Disabilities (NICHCY). (2012). *Categories of disability under IDEA.* Washington, D.C., author. Retrieved from http://nichcy.org/disability/categories#asd

Nunley, K. F. (2006). *Differentiating the high school classroom.* Thousand Oaks, CA: Corwin.

O'Shea, D. J. (1999). Tips for teaching: Making uninvited inclusion work. *Preventing School Failure, 43*(4), 179–181.

Perna, D. M., & Davis, J. R. (2007). *Aligning standards and curriculum for classroom success* (2nd ed.). Thousand Oaks, CA: Corwin.

Provenzo, E. F., Butin, D. W., & Angelini, A. (2008). *100 Experiential Learning Activities for Social Studies, Literature, and the Arts, Grades 5–12*. Thousand Oaks, CA: Corwin.

Reilly, D. H. (2002). The learner centered high school: Prescription for adolescents' success. *Education, 121*(2), 219–228.

Rugutt, J. (2004, Fall). Linking individual and institutional factors to motivation: A multilevel approach. *Journal of Educational Research and Policy Studies, 4*(2), 52–85.

Sabornie, E. J., & deBettencourt, L. U. (2009). *Teaching students with mild and high-incidence disabilities at the secondary level*. Upper Saddle River, NJ: Merrill.

Salend, S. J. (2005). *Creating inclusive classrooms: Effective and reflective practices for all students*. Upper Saddle River, NJ: Pearson.

Saylers, F., & McKee, C. (2002). *The young adolescent learner*. Retrieved March 18, 2012, from http://www.learner.org/workshops/middlewriting/images/pdf/W1ReadAdLearn.pdf

Silberman, M. (1996). *Active learning: 101 strategies to teach any subject*. Needham Heights, MA: Allyn & Bacon.

Silberman, M. (2006). *Teaching actively: Eight steps and thirty-two strategies to spark learning in any classroom*. Boston: Pearson.

Sliva, J. A. (2004). *Teaching inclusive mathematics to special learners, K–6*. Thousand Oaks, CA: Corwin.

Smart, K., & Csapo, N. (2007). Learning by doing: Engaging students through learner centered activities. *Focus on Teaching*, 451–457.

Smith, T. E. C., Palloway, E. A., Patton, J. R., & Dowdy, C. A. (2006). *Teaching students with special needs in inclusive settings*. Boston: Pearson.

Snyder, R. F. (1999). Inclusion: A qualitative study of inservice general education teachers' attitudes and concerns. *Education, 120*(1), 173–180.

Sousa, D. A. (2007). *Brain research into classroom practice*. Retrieved March 18, 2012, from http://www.ldaofmichigan.org/articles/Sousa1-07.htm

Swanson, H. L. (1987). Information processing theory and learning disabilities: An overview. *Journal of Learning Disabilities, 20*, 3–7.

Swanson, H. L. (2001). Research on interventions for adolescents: A meta-analysis of outcomes related to higher order processing. *Elementary School Journal, 101*, 331–349.

Swanson, H. L., & Deshler, D. (2003, March). Instructing adolescents with learning disabilities: Converting a meta-analysis to practice. *Journal of Learning Disabilities, 36*(2), 124–135.

Tomlinson, C. A. (1999). *The differentiated classroom: Responding to the needs of all learners*. Alexandria, VA: Association for Supervision and Curriculum Development.

Tomlinson, C. A., & Allan, S. D. (2000). *Leadership for differentiating schools and classrooms*. Alexandria, VA: Association for Supervision and Curriculum Development.

Udvari-Solner, A., & Kluth, P. (2008). *Joyful learning: Active and collaborative learning in inclusive classrooms*. Thousand Oaks, CA: Corwin.

Uguroglu, M. E., & Walberg, H. J. (1979). Motivation and achievement: A quantitative syntheses. *American Educational Research Journal, 16*(4), 375–390.

Vollmer, J. R. (2002). *The blueberry story*. Retrieved from http://www.jamievollmer.com/blue_story.html

Willis, J. (2006). *Research-based strategies to ignite student learning: Insights from a neurologist and class teacher*. Alexandria, VA: ASCD.

Willis, J. (2007). Cooperative learning is a brain turn-on. *Middle School Journal, 38*(4), 4–13.

Wilson, L. M., & Horch, H. W. (2002). Implications of brain based research for teaching young adolescents. *Middle School Journal, 34*(1), 57–60.

Wood, J. (2009). *Pathways to teaching strategies: Practical strategies for the inclusive classroom*. Upper Saddle River, NJ: Pearson.

Wood, K. (2008). Mathematics through movement: An investigation of the links between kinesthetic and conceptual learning. *Australian Primary Mathematics, 13*(1), 18–22.

Zmuda, A. (2008, November). Springing into active learning. *Educational Leadership, 66*(3), 38–42.

CORWIN
A SAGE Company